THE ART OF LACEMAKING

THE ART OF
LACEMAKING

Ann Collier

BRACKEN BOOKS
LONDON

Acknowledgements
The author and publishers gratefully acknowledge
the assistance of the following companies
and organisations in the preparation of
this book:

J. & P. Coats (UK) Limited
Madeira Threads (UK) Limited
Exeter Museum, Devon
National Portrait Gallery, London

Picture credits
Special photography by Di Lewis
Page 24: Photography 2000
Pages 92-93: J & P Coats (UK) Ltd
Pages 66-67, 80-81: Mary Evans Picture Library
Pages 12-13: The Dick Institute, Kilmarnock
Pages 8-9, 63: Victoria and Albert Museum, London
Pages 26-27, 34-35: Hispanic Society of America
Page 63: Rijksmuseum, Amsterdam
Page 6: Musée Royaux, Brussels
Page 64: Exeter Museum, Devon

Previously published in 1986 by David & Charles Publishers plc,
Newton Abbot

This edition published 1989 by Bracken Books
an imprint of Bestseller Publications Ltd.
Princess House, 50 Eastcastle Street
London W1N 7AP, England

By arrangement with David & Charles Publishers plc

ISBN 1 85170 232 6

Printed and bound in Great Britain
by Camelot Press, Southampton

Edited by Eve Harlow; Book design by Michael Head

CONTENTS

Wedding veil in Point de Gaze lace, made in the nineteenth century (Museé Royaux, Brussels)

The Art of Lacemaking

In its early form, lace was made by withdrawing threads from woven fabrics, then pulling the remaining threads together with stitches to form an intricate pattern of holes. Centuries later, when the first needle laces evolved, they still relied on a drawn fabric ground, but now holes were also cut in the fabric and filled with decorative stitchery. This was generally referred to as Renaissance work and from this the true laces were developed, with their own laid threads, independent of a fabric ground. The true laces began in Italy and the concept was called *Punto in Aria* – 'stitches in the air'.

Lace was made from linen threads and the finest flax was cultivated in the coastal regions of Holland, Belgium and France and, later, in Ireland, Poland and Russia. Belgium was regarded as the centre for bobbin lace, but there was very close liaison between Italy and Belgium, the latter supplying the smooth linen thread to Italy for her needle lace industries. There is strong evidence to suggest that the development from cutwork to Reticella and free needle lace occurred almost simultaneously in the two countries.

The needle laces differed in style from area to area – coarse and heavy, light and dainty, floral, geometric – as fashion dictated. It was a skilfully-made product, treasured like jewellery and, in fact, cost almost as much. Lace was bought only by the very wealthy and, when worn in society, was regarded as an emblem of prestige.

Italian lace

The Renaissance brought great wealth to Italy and the Venetian style of lace was favoured throughout Europe. The heavy Venetian Gros Point was used for collars and neckbands and this sculptured lace, with its designs of stylised flowers and scrolls, echoed the grandiose style in architecture and furnishings. Even the churches were lavishly furnished with lace, devoted women spending years of their lives making lace to adorn altars, statues – and the priests.

Throughout the seventeenth century, the lace industry flourished, but nowhere as much as it did in Italy, with Venice regarded as the centre of trade.

Almost every European country was importing lace from Italy. It was very expensive and, because of its prestige value, everyone of note was anxious to own some, no matter how little. Import taxes were high, because most European countries had their own lace industries and it was economically important to discourage the vast sums being spent in Italy on lace. This, of course, led to smuggling and it was amazing the lengths people would go to indulge their passion for lace. It came into countries in coffins, wrapped around the corpses of expatriates, or wound around small pet dogs, which were swaddled in fur wraps in attempts to avoid detection. The penalties for smuggling lace were heavy but the commodity was so valuable that

Point de Gaze fan

many thought the risk worth taking.

By the 1660s some European countries were experiencing economic difficulties over the amount of money being spent abroad on lace.

Colbert, Minister of Finance to Louis XIV, determined to stop the vast amounts of money leaving France, recommended that the government should support and develop the French lace industry. The best lacemakers from Italy and Belgium were encouraged to settle in France and schools were set up in the established lace areas of Alençon, Arras and Sedan. Alençon and Argentan were small towns close to each other, and it was here that the revival of French lace was to occur.

A new lace – Point de France

At first, the designs of the lace produced by the Italian immigrants were

similar to the Venetian lace but, before long, an entirely new lace was being produced – softer, with many more filling stitches and altogether of a very ornate and luxurious appearance. Point de France was an almost immediate success, particularly with the Court of Louis XIV. Fashion style was changing and there was demand for softer, more supple laces, to be worn as cravats, wrist falls, collars, apron fronts and ruffles.

Italy, realising that her lacemaking industry was at stake, issued an edict which read: 'If any artist or craftsman practises his art in a foreign land, to the detriment of the Republic, orders will be sent for his return. If he disobeys, his nearest kin will be imprisoned. If he returns, employment will be found for him.'

France allowed the Venetian lacemakers to return to Italy but they had served their purpose and Point de France achieved a supreme position in Europe.

Both Alençon lace and Argentan lace were in great demand. Sometimes the lace techniques of these two were combined to make a beautiful, textured lace, and fine horsehair was used as padding on the outside edges to give designs a crisper outline.

Fashion changes

The classic period for both bobbin lace and needle lace was the eighteenth century. Thread was at its finest and the techniques were fully developed. Needle lace tended to be rather stiff in texture and, with fashion demanding a soft, draped look, it began to fall from favour towards the end of the century. Bobbin lace began to come into its heyday.

Needle lace producers countered by grounding their laces on a light mesh, and sometimes combined needle lace and bobbin lace. Cotton threads were beginning to replace the stiffer, linen threads, and softer laces were possible. By 1764, background net could be made on a machine.

The Revolution at the end of the eighteenth century brought an end to the over-indulgent era in France and the lace industry suffered in the extreme. The 1800s also brought a new fashion line, with almost no emphasis on lace and, as France always led fashion, the new styles were quickly adopted throughout Europe. The new look was neo-classical, with muslin and other diaphanous fabrics in demand, and this too, was calamitous for the lace industries because machines could now produce net, or tulle, as it was

Part of a Point de France border, made in France in the late seventeenth century (Victoria and Albert Museum, London. Crown Copyright)

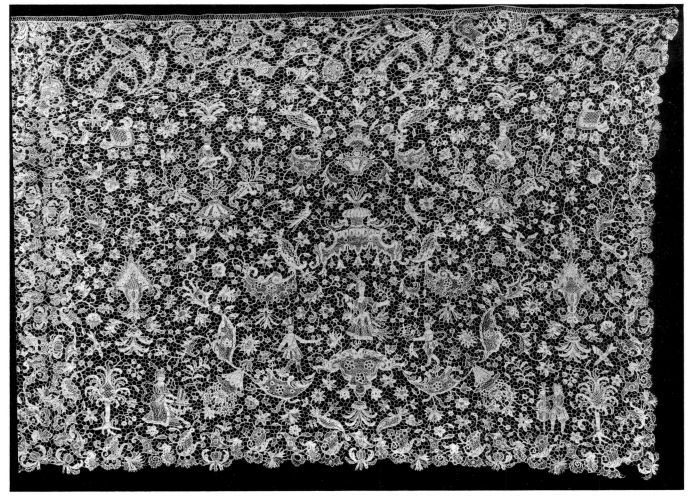

Dresden work: corner of a handkerchief, eighteenth century

called. The lace industry throughout Europe was affected and was never again to be in the position it was in before the French Revolution.

The early part of the nineteenth century was a bleak one for the lace industry and its workers. There was constant competition between hand-made and machine-made laces because the machines could produce good copies of most laces and they were far cheaper.

Nineteenth-century revival

However, there was a growing society of the industrial rich and their attitude to lace was encouraging. Male costume was austere but it was different for the women. Fashion designers began to look back to the sumptuous, extravagant styles of the seventeenth century and a demand began to grow for the old laces. This produced its own difficulties because, by this time, there were very few

skilled workers and so the lace schools were re-opened for training. French lacemakers were encouraged to go to Burano in Northern Italy to revive the needle lace industry there, because the art had been lost – a reversal of the situation when Colbert had encouraged the Italian lacemakers to go to France.

The old styles and designs were reproduced but, in some cases, were not as exquisite as the originals because the threads used were no longer so fine and the workers so skilled, but some of the Alençon and Brussels needle points produced in this period were superb.

From 1840, lace was worn by almost every class in society, only now it did not have a prestige value – it was just part of everyday fashion. Much of it was machine-made but it was still possible to buy hand-made laces in the established lacemaking centres.

New laces were developed and the most distinctive was Point de Gaze, made in Belgium and exhibited at a trade fair for the first time in 1847. It

was highly successful, with designs that resembled paintings and shadings worked in stitchery. The effect was quite outstanding. The 'boom' in lace continued through to the end of the century, with the Victorians wearing enormous amounts of lace. Dresses had collars and undersleeves; accessories, such as shawls, fans, kerchiefs, hat veils and gloves, etc, were lavishly trimmed with lace. Home furnishings also, tablecloths, antimacassars, and bed linens, all had lace trims. Every surface that could be covered with a cloth had a lace border of some kind.

Into the next century

By the turn of the century, however, lace was once more in a decline, with minimal revivals in the Art Nouveau period and again in the 1920s.

Through the 1930s to the Second World War, lace continued to be produced in peasant communities, and in the European lace centres as a tourist attraction. In the last few years, here at the end of the twentieth century, lacemaking is enjoying a revival again, but this time as a leisure activity. Crochet, macramé and tatting were the first to emerge, followed by an interest in bobbin lacemaking. Now there is an interest in needlemade lace again and many designers are developing new trends in dimensional and coloured work, using the newly-available coloured and textured threads.

The Lace Guild of England was formed in 1976 and its members have interest in all types of lace. A Needle Lace Guild has also formed, with interest in all kinds of needle lace. An International Organisation for the promotion of bobbin lacemaking and needle lace was set up in Belgium in 1982 and its membership is worldwide. Techniques, designs and ideas are exchanged between members from different countries and some countries without lace traditions, such as Japan and Australia, are becoming members.

Lace is moving out of a decline into new, creative areas and perhaps this ancient craft will continue to grow into the twenty-first century.

I hope that this book will go some way into making you want to explore the romance and mystery of lace, and perhaps to want to join those millions of lacemakers who, over the centuries, have contributed to this beautiful art form.

Glossary of Lacemaking

Alençon — French needle lace with a light, twisted net ground.

Argentan — French needle lace with a hexagonal, buttonhole-stitched mesh ground.

Bars — Whipped or Buttonhole-stitched threads.

Bobbin lace — Lace made by plaiting and weaving threads with the use of bobbins, worked on a cushion or pillow.

Branscombe point — A tape lace developed in 1860, in Devon, England.

Buttonhole stitch — The basic stitch used in making needle lace.

Buttonhole-stitched rings — These are also called 'Couronnes'.

Cambric — Very fine, almost transparent, woven cotton fabric.

Chantilly — A straight lace, made in silk thread, with an outline of coarse thread.

Cordonnet — The raised edge of needle lace.

Couronnes — Buttonhole-stitched rings.

Crochet — The French word for the hooked needle used in lacemaking. Also describes an openwork construction formed by looping threads with a hook.

Cutwork — Needle lace based on a woven fabric ground.

Drawn thread work — An embroidery technique where threads are withdrawn from fabric to form an open base for embroidery.

Dresden work — An elaborate form of white embroidery and pulled work, made to resemble bobbin lace.

Edging — Lace with one straight edge, formed to be applied to fabric.

Embroidered lace — Net worked with embroidery stitches and fancy darning patterns.

Filet — French for Lacis, a term used for hand-knotted square net.

Fillings — Composite stitches worked to form a decorative pattern.

Greek lace — A needle lace of the Italian type, worked in the nineteenth century.

Gros Point — A term used to describe the largest patterns in Venetian needle lace.

Ground — The background net of all laces.

Guipure — A nineteenth-century term for lace without a net background but with buttonhole-stitched bars.

Hollie Point — Small-scale insertions of knotted needle lace made in the eighteenth century in England.

Insertion — A piece of lace intended for inserting into a piece of fabric. Some, or all the sides of a piece of lace are attached to the right side of fabric, then the fabric is cut away behind the lace.

Lacis — A ancient technique for producing hand-knotted net.

Lappets — Hanging strips of lace, which were attached to women's caps.

Lawn — Fine, evenly-woven fabric, usually cotton.

Lille — A French straight lace.

Limerick — Decorated, machine-made net.

Macramé — An ancient technique of knotting in decorative patterns.

Medici collar — High-standing collar with a front opening.

Mesh — The basic element of a piece of net.

Muslin — Semi-transparent cotton fabric.

Nanduti — Rounds or wheels in needle-weaving from South America.

Needle lace — Openwork constructed stitch-upon-stitch with needle and thread.

Needle point — Another term for needle lace.

Needle run — Decoration of machine-made net with darning.

Net — Alternative word for mesh.

Picot — French for 'peak', small projections of loops or knots decorating lace.

Point — French term meaning 'stitch'. Also, a needle lace term indentifying the country of origin.

Point lace — A term for tape lace with needle-made fillings, worked in the nineteenth century.

Point de France — French needle lace, produced from 1665.

Point de Gaze — Nineteenth-century name for a new form of Brussels needle lace.

Point de Neige — The finest of the Venetian needle point laces.

Pulled work — Describes the technique where threads of fabric are pulled together to form holes.

Punto — Italian term for 'point'.

Punto in Aria — 'Stitches in the air', or freely-formed needle lace.

Reticella — Geometric cutwork of the late sixteenth century.

Rose Point — Name given to a medium-sized Venetian Point lace.

Ruff — Wheel-shaped collar, often quite deep, pleated to surround the neck.

Sol lace — Spanish form of cutwork and drawn thread work in a wheel formation.

Straight lace — Lace made in one piece.

Tape lace — Lace constructed from a machine- or hand-made braid.

Tracing linen — Stiffened linen, usually pale blue, used by architects and draughtsmen, and used for tracing needle lace patterns.

Tatting — Lacemaking technique where a continuous thread is wound onto a shuttle, and is then knotted and looped to form rings decorated with picots.

Teneriffe lace — A version of Sol lace constructed on a framework of laid threads.

Tulle — A town in France that gave its name to a very fine net, often made of silk.

Youghal — The most important of needle lace centres in Ireland.

CHAPTER ONE

LACE FROM WOVEN FABRIC

The starting point for this type of work was linen fabric. Linen is the most ancient of all materials and its fibre produced a smooth lustrous thread which bleached easily in the sun and made a supple cloth on the simplest of looms. It was used for both dress and furnishing, and rich decoration became desirable to make its rather plain weave more interesting.

People have always been interested in creating lace-like fabrics and found many ways of achieving them. Because of its loose, even weave, the threads of linen could be pulled together to make open patterns and surface embroidery added, warp and weft threads could be cut out and the square holes filled with open stitchery, or holes could be punched into eyelets and overcast.

Cotton was introduced into Europe in the seventeenth century and by the eighteenth century both linen and cotton fibres could be spun extremely finely and woven to create a diaphanous fabric. This fine muslin could be pulled and embroidered into a lacy fabric which was hardly distinguishable from bobbin lace. It was much cheaper to produce than bobbin lace as the skills required were not so specialised. More people could use a needle than could handle a bobbin.

As fashions changed, new ways of combining these methods developed and by the 1840s white work embroidery, combined with pulled and cut work, was used extensively for decorating day dresses as well as for small pieces such as collars, undersleeves, caps etc. Far out-numbering these were the baby gowns which were carefully preserved from generation to generation. Most of this work was carried out in workrooms in Scotland providing a much needed industry for the area; it was commonly called Ayrshire work or Scotch Hole. 'Kits' of embroidered pieces were supplied for the amateur to put together and many needlewomen worked their own pieces since embroidery of all kinds was considered a ladylike pursuit.

Scottish cottager, Mrs Paisley, late nineteenth century

Richelieu or Italian Cutwork

Cutwork is a form of embroidery where the embroidery is completed and then parts of the fabric are cut away. Holes are overcast on the edges and Buttonhole stitch is worked with the knots lying towards the edges where the fabric is to be cut away. Larger holes are linked with Buttonhole-stitched bars.

Cutwork, as a lace form, became increasingly popular in the sixteenth century – portraits of the time show both men and women wearing collars and kerchiefs and with sleeves made of cutwork – and gentlewomen worked the embroidery as a pleasant pastime.

During the seventeenth and eighteenth centuries, when linen weaving reached a peak, the fineness of the cloth produced an even higher quality of cutwork, the firmness of the

Richelieu or Italian cutwork used to make a modern windowblind

woven fabric providing the embroiderer with a suitable ground on which to work. As the holes were filled with more complex stitchery, cutwork developed into Reticella.

Although the technique was known in most European countries, including Greece, and is known to have been worked in Mexico also, the type of cutwork known as Richelieu was developed in France during the time of Cardinal Richelieu, in the seventeenth century. The French government was becoming concerned about the large quantities of Venetian lace being imported into the country and encouraged the embroiderers to produce a cutwork version of the lace. The scrolling forms were outlined on fine linen, the shapes then Buttonhole-stitched and the fabric cut away, the design being held with worked bars and Spider Fillings. From a distance, the effect resembled Gros Point but was, of course, much cheaper to produce. The fashionable French however, considered Richelieu work a poor substitute for Venetian lace, and the embroidery was never really popular in France.

The embroidery experienced a revival two hundred years later in

Victorian England and enjoyed considerable popularity, used on household linens, furnishings and on small items of clothing.

The piece used for a blind in the picture dates from the nineteenth century and probably started out as a chair back, or 'throw', for upholstered furniture. The design, of birds and beasts, is typical of the earlier French designs and a single bird has been abstracted for you to work (Fig 1, page 16). The motif could be used as an insert for a tablecloth or a traycloth, or could be worked as a decoration for a window blind. The finished motif is approximately 20cm (8in) square and could also be used to decorate a large lampshade. When used for a lampshade, the open-work motif creates a striking focal point in a dark corner, with light shining through the lace.

Motifs for Richelieu cutwork
Motifs and patterns for this technique can also be obtained from embroidery transfers. Providing areas of the pattern join one another, almost any design is possible – floral, pictorial, geometric or abstract – and this provides you with scope for practising the technique.

Detail from the nineteenth-century piece from which the Bird and Flowers panel has been designed

BIRD AND FLOWERS
PANEL

Materials required

30cm (12in) square of firm, fine
  fabric, linen or cotton
1 ball of matching Coton à Broder, or
  Swedish linen thread; (stranded
  embroidery cotton can also be
  used, match the number of strands
  to the weight of a single thread of
  fabric)
A needle and a sharp, pointed pair of
  embroidery scissors are also
  required.

Fig 1 *The Bird and Flower panel. Use as a life-
sized trace-off pattern*

16

Preparation for working

Trace the design (Fig 1) on stiff tracing paper, using a hard (2H) pencil. Pencil over the design lines on the reverse side, using a soft (2B) pencil. Take care to follow the design lines accurately.

Place the traced design on the right side of the fabric, with the right side of the tracing facing up. Pin the tracing to the fabric. Place the fabric on a hard surface and draw over the design lines with a sharp, hard pencil.

Working the technique

Having removed the tracing and checked that all the design lines are clear on the fabric, work a line of running stitches between all the double design lines. When you reach a bar (Fig 2), carry the running thread across to the opposite double line and work 3 or 4 long stitches. Work Buttonhole stitches along the bar. If the bar has a branch (Fig 3), when you reach that point, work long stitches to make the branched bar, and cover this also with close Buttonhole stitches. Continue working the remainder of the bar (Fig 4). Make sure that the Buttonhole stitches do not catch the fabric under the bars because the fabric underneath these will be cut away later. If you would like to add further embellishment with Spider Fillings (Fig 5), work these now.

When the bars have been worked, work close Buttonhole stitches over all the double design lines, with the knots lying to the edges were fabric is to be cut away.

Work the stamens of the flowers in a padded Satin stitch, and work a ring of Buttonhole stitches round the bird's eye.

Flowers can be varied by using groups of French Knots in the centres. Other embroidery stitches can be added to the bird's wing and tail for textural interest.

Finishing

When the embroidery is completed, cut away the fabric up to the Buttonhole-stitched edges, taking care that you do not snip into the embroidery. Cut the fabric away beneath the bars. If the embroidery requires pressing, do this on the wrong side with the embroidery lying on a soft, padded surface.

Another detail from the blind on page 14. Trace the motif with double lines, drawing in lines for bars, to prepare a trace-off pattern

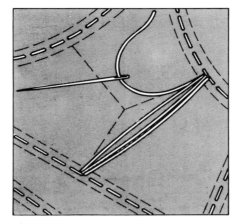

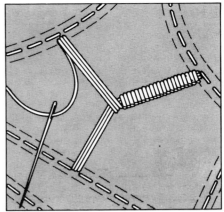

Fig 2 *Work long, straight stitches between double design lines to work the bars*

Fig 3 *Work close Buttonhole stitches over the threads to form bars. If a branched bar is reached, work straight stitches for the branch*

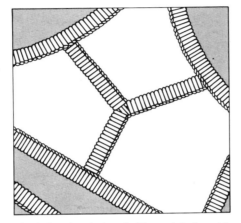

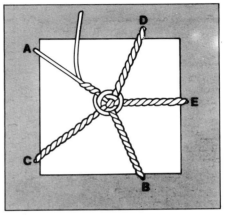

Fig 4 *Complete the branched bar and the bar with close Buttonhole stitches*

Fig 5 *Spider Filling: Work overcasting over the five threads of the Filling*

Broderie Anglaise

This open form of embroidery is also known as Ayrshire, English, Scotch Hole, Madeira or Swiss work. To obtain the 'lace' effect, holes of varying sizes are cut or punched with a stiletto in cotton or linen fabric, the edges of the holes being overcast in Satin stitch or Buttonhole stitch. Broderie Anglaise is usually finished on the edges with scallops of padded Buttonhole stitches.

The classic period of Broderie anglaise was in the late eighteenth and nineteenth centuries. It was used extensively for underclothes, caps, undersleeves and for baby gowns. The holes were round or oval in shape and lent themselves well to the floral designs that were so popular.

The baby gown in the picture is a typical design of the mid-nineteenth century, with patterning on the triangular front bodice, the sleeves, and on the panelled skirt. The design is continued round the scalloped hem. Some of the holes have been further decorated with a needle filling.

Triangular-shaped bodices were very common and echoed the designs of adult dresses. The bodice was left as a triangle for a boy, but tucked in for a girl.

The shaped piece, abstracted from

Mid-nineteenth century baby gown from which the triangular pattern and edging is abstracted

Detail showing the triangular front panel

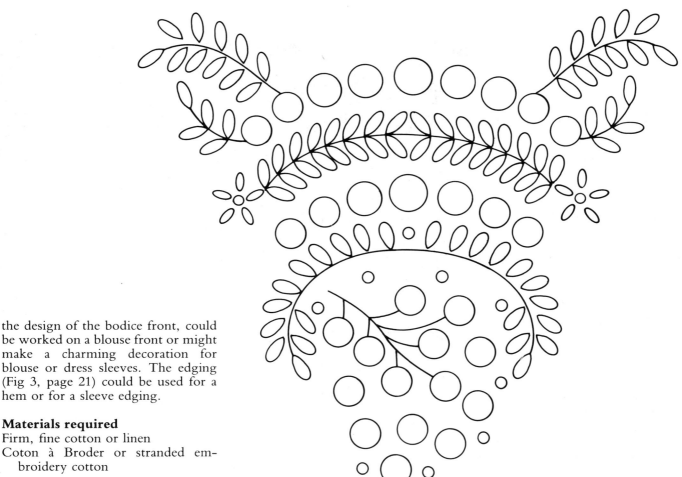

the design of the bodice front, could be worked on a blouse front or might make a charming decoration for blouse or dress sleeves. The edging (Fig 3, page 21) could be used for a hem or for a sleeve edging.

Materials required
Firm, fine cotton or linen
Coton à Broder or stranded embroidery cotton

Preparation for working
Trace the patterns (Fig 1 this page and Fig 3 page 21). Using dressmaker's carbon paper, trace the design (Fig 1) to the right side of fabric.

Work running stitches round all the details of the design. Small holes are pierced with a stiletto (Fig 2). Cut larger holes and ovals with small, sharp, pointed scissors (Fig 3). Overcast the edges of all the holes. Work Buttonhole stitch over the overcasting round the large holes for extra firmness.

Working the edging
Trace the design (Fig 3, page 21) and transfer it along the edge of fabric, moving the tracing for each repeat and taking care to match the edges of the design. Position the tracing so that there is an extra 12mm (½in) above and below the design. Work the holes as described for the triangular-shaped pattern. Pad the scalloped edge with Chain stitch and then finish the edge with Buttonhole stitches (Fig 4). Cut away the excess fabric from the scallops.

Fig 1 *Trace-off for the triangular front panel*

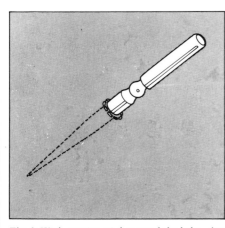

Fig 2 *Work running stitches round the holes, then pierce the fabric with a stiletto*

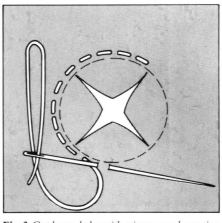

Fig 3 *Cut larger holes with scissors, work running stitches round the holes then overcast the edges*

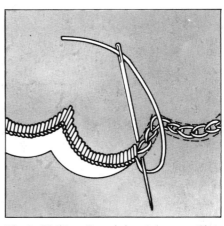

Fig 4 *Working Buttonhole stitch over Chain stitches, worked along the scallops to pad the edge*

Bonnets and Caps

The head has always been an important area to cover, either for protection or for decoration.

In the sixteenth century, babies' caps were tight and came well over their ears, and were believed to help the skull to close.

The heads of both women and girls were always covered and it was usual for them to wear small linen caps indoors and more decorative ones outside. Linen caps were also worn at night to protect the head from cold draughts. By the end of the nineteenth century children were less formally dressed, and their clothing was less restrictive, but hats and caps were still worn. Bonnets for little girls, like the one in the picture, were always made of fabric and it was not until the twentieth century that baby bonnets were knitted from wool.

The bonnet dates from the late nineteenth century and was made for a young child. It has areas of cutwork combined with Broderie Anglaise and would make a charming cap for a small bridesmaid.

Materials required
30cm (12in) square of cotton fabric
Matching Coton à Broder or stranded embroidery cotton
Sewing thread

Preparation for working
Trace the pattern shapes for the bonnet (Figs 1 and 2). Using dressmaker's carbon paper (or, if preferred, the soft pencil method described on pages 16–17), transfer the outlines and the decorative pattern to the fabric. Fig 1 is the back and crown of the bonnet. Fig 2 is the pattern for a side – trace this down twice, reversing the pattern once. Make sure A-B lies on the straight grain of fabric.

Working the design
Work the embroidery before cutting out the shapes. Work running stitches round all the design lines. Pierce the holes with a stiletto. Overcast the round and oval holes closely. Work the scrolled lines and flower stems in close Satin stitch. Work the round, flower buds in Satin stitch. The curved, open areas should be worked using the cutwork technique (see pages 16–17). Buttonhole-stitch the edges closely, working bars as indicated by the straight, linking lines. Make sure the stitches do not go through the fabric as the fabric is cut away later.

Edging
The holes at the edges of the bonnet are worked with overcasting on the inner edge, and close Buttonhole stitch on the outside edge, making a scalloped effect.

Finishing
Cut away the fabric under the cutwork carefully. Cut the scalloped edge carefully. Cut out the bonnet pieces. A 9mm (⅜in) seam allowance has been included for making up. Sew or machine-stitch the bonnet together, using run and fell seams.

The little bonnet would make a charming cap for a small bridesmaid

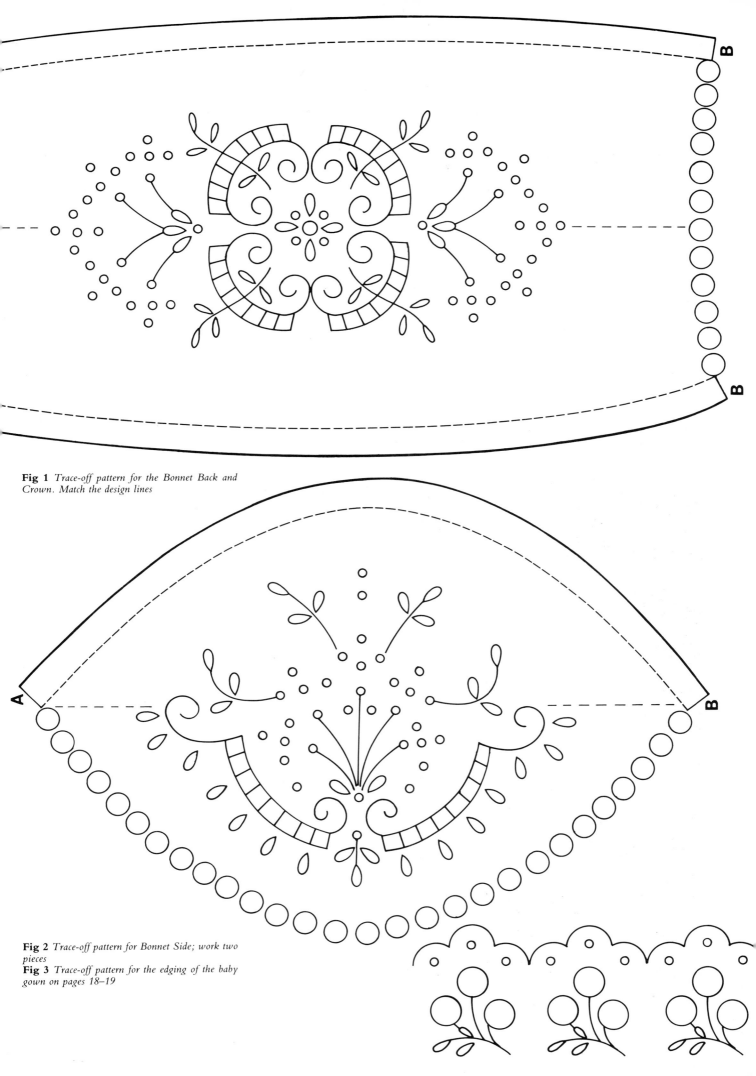

Fig 1 *Trace-off pattern for the Bonnet Back and Crown. Match the design lines*

Fig 2 *Trace-off pattern for Bonnet Side; work two pieces*

Fig 3 *Trace-off pattern for the edging of the baby gown on pages 18–19*

Victorian Collars

The collars pictured are Victorian broderie Anglaise and would probably have had undersleeves to match. Both collars can be worked from the trace-off patterns, using the techniques described on pages 18–19 for working the baby gown patterns.

Victorian dresses were made of rich, but non-washable materials so it was important to have those parts of garments in touch with the body – necklines, sleeves, vestees – made of launderable fabric.

Preparation for working
Peter Pan collar Half of the collar is given as a pattern. Trace the pattern twice from Fig 1 and transfer to fabric.

Point-edged collar Half of the collar is given in the pattern. Trace the pattern from Fig 2 and then turn the pattern to trace the other half, taking care to match the design. Transfer the entire collar pattern to fabric.

Working the designs
Peter Pan collar Work running stitch round all the holes. Pierce the holes with a stiletto and cut the larger holes with sharp pointed scissors. Overcast all the holes in the design. Buttonhole-stitch the holes on the edges of the collar.

Point-edged collar Work running stitches round all the holes shapes. Pierce the round holes with a stiletto. Cut the oval and larger holes with scissors. Overcast the edges of the holes on the inner design areas. Buttonhole-stitch the holes on the edges of the collar. Work the small flower buds in padded Satin stitch.

Finishing
Cut out the collars to the broken line which indicates the dress neck edge. Cut round the collar edges carefully. Bind the neck edges of the two Peter Pan collar pieces and the neckline of the point-edged collar with bias-cut strips of the same fabric.

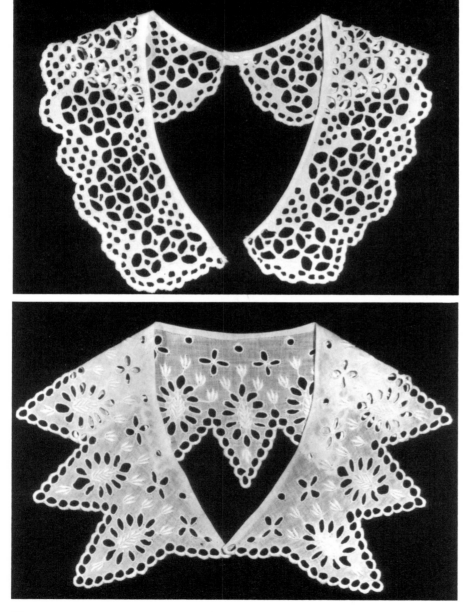

Peter Pan collar in broderie Anglaise

Point-edged collar in broderie Anglaise

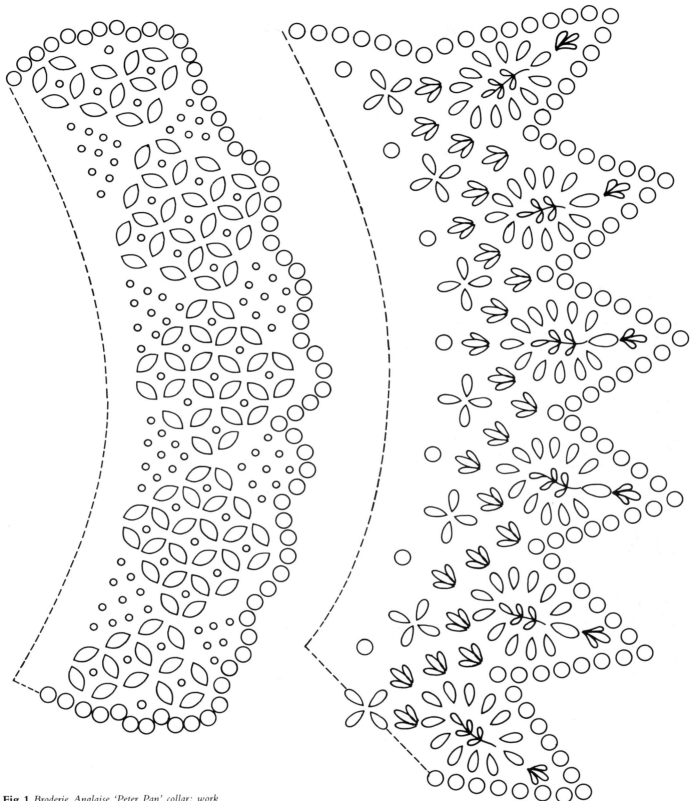

Fig 1 *Broderie Anglaise 'Peter Pan' collar; work two pieces*

Fig 2 *Broderie Anglaise point-edged collar; trace the half given and re-trace to obtain a pattern for the whole collar*

23

Ayrshire Embroidery

Ayrshire embroidery is the name given to a whitework embroidery, worked on fine muslin or cambric. An industry for producing the delicate work was set up in Ayr in Scotland in 1820 by the wife of a Mr Jamieson, a cotton agent.

Mrs Jamieson and her two daughters instructed a group of women workers in the art of embroidery and the making of the delicate fillings that are characteristic of this work. The designs were drawn by professional draughtsmen, and workers made the part of the design at which they were considered most skilled. The best embroideresses received the highest wages.

The production of Ayrshire embroidery became a thriving industry in an otherwise impoverished area and the lace was widely marketed and exported.

By the end of the 1830s, stamped designs were being sent to outworkers all over Scotland and Northern Ireland, and 'kits' were prepared for the home needlewoman. The invention of the Swiss embroidery machine saw the end of hand-worked Ayrshire embroidery as an industry and the craft had more or less died out by the turn of the century.

The baby bonnet pictured is a typical example of Ayrshire embroidery worked around 1850. The bonnet is of fine muslin with the front edge able to be drawn up to fit with a fine cord, and edged with lace. The design is a repeat pattern of flowers, and the bonnet crown is lavishly decorated with cutwork and fillings.

The detail (opposite page) shows a motif from the bonnet which could be worked using modern threads, and used as appliqué or as an insert on lingerie, blouses or on baby garments.

Materials required
Fine cotton lawn
Stranded embroidery cotton (match the number of stranded cotton threads used to the thickness of one thread of the fabric)

Preparing to work
Trace the design (Fig 1) and transfer to the fabric, using dressmaker's carbon paper.

Working the design
Work running stitches round all the design lines.

Work the leaves in padded Satin stitch.

Work the stems in Stem stitch.

Pierce the eyelets in the flower with a stiletto and overcast the edges closely (see pages 18–19, Fig 2, for technique). Cut out the larger holes in the flowers and overcast the edges closely.

When the surface embroidery is completed, baste the fabric to a piece of firm paper (brown wrapping paper is a suitable weight). Baste round the large flower holes also.

Filling stitches
The needle filling stitches most commonly used in Ayrshire work are Twisted Buttonhole stitch and Double Twisted Buttonhole stitch.

In Buttonhole stitch, the thread from the previous stitch is under the needle. In Twisted Buttonhole stitch, the thread from the needle eye is under the needle (Fig 2a). Begin at the base of the calyx.

1st row Following Fig 2a and 2b, and using a single thread of stranded cotton, work Twisted Buttonhole stitch, setting the stitches into the Satin stitched edge and working from left to right.

Work the stitches over the surface of the supporting paper. When the right hand edge is reached, take the thread under, then over, the edge, ready to work the second row.

The baby bonnet is a typical example of Ayrshire whitework embroidery, probably worked around 1850. Cutwork and intricate fillings decorate the crown, with a pretty repeat pattern of flowers worked in bands

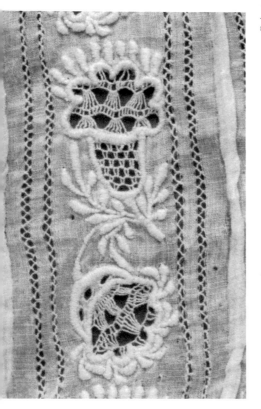

blocks of the stitch forming long loops. Fig 3 shows that the stitch is worked by taking the thread from the needle eye twice round the needle from left to right.

1st row Working from the top of the flower, work two blocks of 4 Double Twisted Buttonhole stitches, with a space between.

2nd row Whip back along the stitches, whipping over the Satin stitched edge to bring the thread into position for the third row.

3rd row Work a row of evenly-spaced Twisted Buttonhole stitches, alternating them between the Double Twists and the spaces.

4th row Whip back to the left.

5th row Work 4 Double Twisted Buttonhole stitches into the spaces, so that they lie below the 4 blocks of the previous row. Miss 4 spaces and repeat to the end.

Repeat these rows and then attach the last row to the base of the flower head.

Finishing
Remove the basting stitches to release the work from the paper. Press the lace on the wrong side, over a soft, padded surface.

Fig 1 *Trace-off pattern for the motif*

2nd row Whip the thread over and under loops (Fig 2b), until the left hand edge is reached. Take the thread under and then over the edge.

3rd row Repeat the first row, placing the stitches in the spaces of the previous row.

Continue working rows in the same way until the area is filled, catching the stitches of the last row into the Satin stitched edge.

Double Twisted Buttonhole stitch This is used for the flower heads, with four

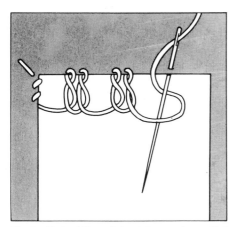

Fig 2a *Twisted Buttonhole stitch, sometimes called Tulle stitch: 1st row, work stitches with the needle towards the body, taking the thread round the needle from left to right*

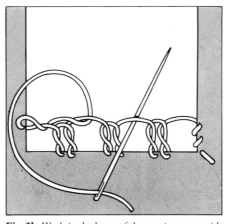

Fig 2b *Work in the loops of the previous row with the work turned and the needle away from the body. For an open Tulle stitch in large areas, take the thread through a small basted stitch before working the Buttonhole stitch*

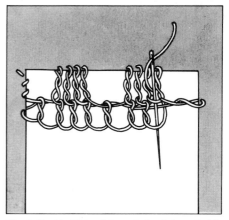

Fig 3 *Double Twisted Buttonhole stitch worked in blocks of four with a row of Tulle stitch in between*

25

CHAPTER TWO

LACE FROM EVENWEAVE FABRIC

Drawn thread work is probably the earliest form of lace and is a comparatively simple technique involving withdrawing some threads from fabric and working embroidery on those that are left. Drawn thread work relies upon an evenweave construction and, therefore, designs are usually geometric.

Most of the garments worn in the early centuries were made from square or rectangular pieces of cloth and it was a simple matter to withdraw threads parallel to the edges. Drawn thread embroidery was a common form of decoration on robes, shirts and chemises, and on household linens.

Drawn thread and cutwork

Over the centuries, many countries have evolved their own forms of drawn thread work and there has been considerable exchange of design ideas. Italy, for instance, specialised in a combination of drawn thread work and cutwork. Greek embroiderers copied the concept as Greek Lace.

The same combination of techniques was picked up by the British artist John Ruskin during a trip to Italy. A leading activist in the nineteenth-century crafts revival, Ruskin encouraged local women in Cumberland to spin and weave imported Belgian flax. The linen was decorated with cutwork and drawn thread work and is now called Ruskin lace.

In Spain, a distinctive form of drawn thread work evolved. Basically, the technique still involved working on a framework of threads but, at corners where withdrawn threads left a hole, or where holes were cut in the fabric, new threads were added in a radial wheel formation. Needle-weaving worked on the wheel produced intricate 'sun' patterns and the embroidery became known as Sol lace. The pattern technique spread to Spain's colonies and, soon, South America, then Madeira and Teneriffe, were producing Sol lace.

Canary Islanders working on a drawn-work bedspread. Early twentieth century

Drawn thread Lace

Fabrics with an even weave, made of cotton linen or linen-type fibres, are used for drawn thread work. The embroidery is worked with thread similar in weight and colour to the thread withdrawn from the fabric. Stranded embroidery cotton, lace thread or, for pure linen, Swedish linen threads, are all suitable.

It is sometimes possible to use threads withdrawn from the fabric to work the embroidery, but test the strength of the thread first. These added threads are used to group threads together. By pulling threads tightly, designs of holes can be made.

Withdrawing threads from fabric

Select the position of the drawn thread insert and count threads to find the centre weft thread. Follow this to the selvedges and cut the thread free at both ends. Lift the thread with a needle point and pull it out.

Cut threads on either side and withdraw them, as desired, in the same way.

To make a hem on a garment or house linen, leave the hem's width, and withdraw the first thread above. Withdraw other threads, as desired, above this first thread.

Plan the position of the hem on the fabric, then withdraw threads to a depth of 12mm (½in).

Work Hemstitching along both edges (Figs 1a and 1b). To complete the hem, draw threads together in groups of three, using Coral stitch (Fig 2).

Decorative insert

Fig 3 illustrates how threads are drawn together in clusters. Withdraw threads from the fabric to a depth of 31mm (1¼in). Hemstitch the edges (Figs 1a and 1b).

Group the threads together in fours, alternating on top and bottom edges, and held with Coral stitches (Fig 3).

For the next stage, start new threads at points A (Fig 3) and work a Coral stitch at the intersections.

Start new threads at B and work Coral stitches at the intersections of the threads from A. Start new threads at C and work to the end.

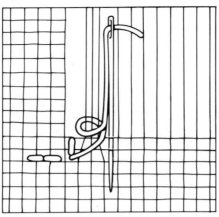

Fig 1a *Hemstitching: Fasten the thread end at the left of the fabric. Take the needle round 3 vertical threads, bring needle through from the back, 2 fabric threads down*

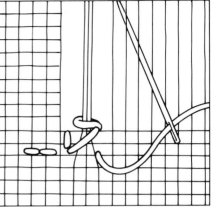

Fig 1b *To make the next stitch, take the needle round the next 3 threads, ready to bring through from the back 2 fabric threads down*

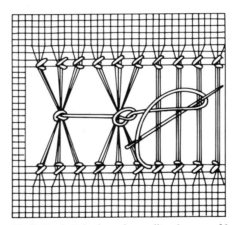

Fig 2 *Coral stitch, shown here pulling 3 groups of 3 fabric threads together. Work stitch left to right*

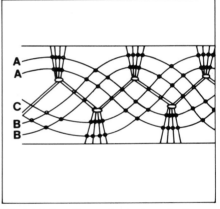

Fig 3 *Working diagram for the decorative insert*

This detail is from the tablecloth on page 30, and shows the effect of the decorative insert. Fig 3 shows how the new threads are introduced

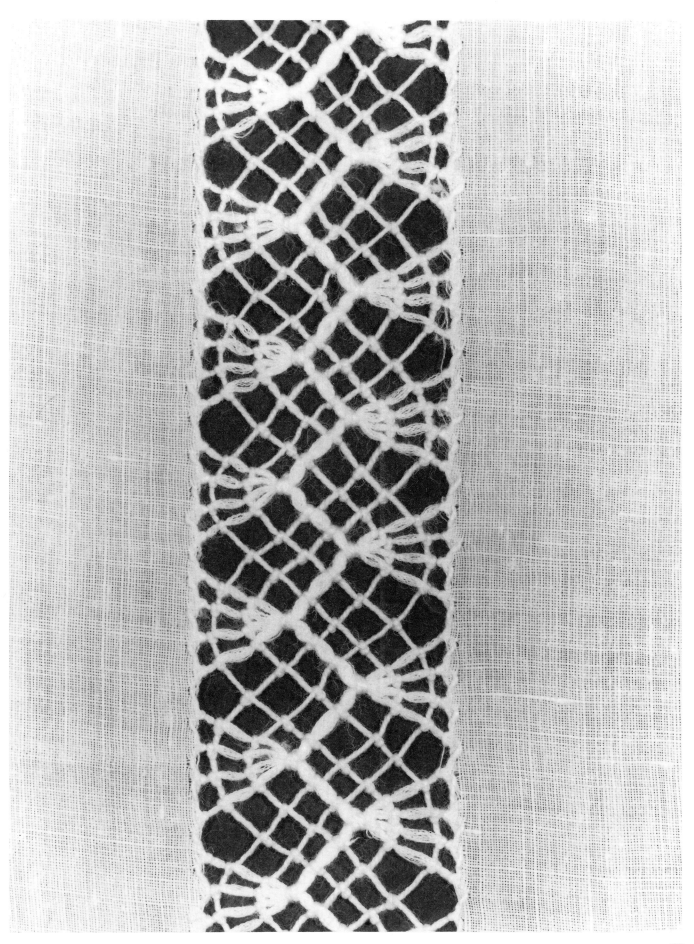

Sol or Ruedas Lace

Sol or Ruedas lace has a distinctive wheel formation. Although the lace is worked on a framework of vertical and horizontal threads, these are pulled into bars and other threads added, until the woven foundation disappears into a dense, needlemade pattern. The large holes, formed by withdrawing both warp and weft threads, have threads laid in a wheel spoke formation and are woven with a needle and thread in a circular movement. By introducing new threads in this way, bright colours could also be used in a design and this was not uncommon in Sol lace.

Sometimes, square areas were cut in the fabric and these also had new threads added and embroidered to make circles. This circular formation, within a square, produced a lacy fabric with an appearance not unlike the geometric cutwork of Italy and Flanders. Sol or Ruedas decoration was widely used for vestments, altar cloths and frontals, as well as for shirts, dresses and other types of clothing.

The tablecloth in the picture is nineteenth century and was almost certainly made in Madeira or Teneriffe. The fabric is fine lawn and the tablecloth border has a pattern of Spider Fillings, Clover Leaves and Suns. Twenty different Sun designs appear on the cloth.

The detail (this page) illustrates one Sun which has been adapted for a design and which can be used on table linen as an insert, or could be extended to fit along the edges of a cloth.

Materials required
Closely-woven, evenweave fabric
Embroidery threads: Choose from Coton à Broder; Coton perlé; Swedish linen thread; fine, bobbin lace thread

Preparation for working
Plan the position of the insert on the fabric. It should be positioned at least 25mm (1in) from the hem edge. The

Nineteenth-century tablecloth, made in either Madeira or Teneriffe

Detail from the cloth, showing a corner

insert should be planned to be at least 37mm (1½in) wide.

Cut through the warp threads at the corner for 37mm (1½in). Cut the weft threads in the same way. Cut the fabric at B (see Fig 2) and withdraw all the cut threads.

Hemstitch both edges (Figs 1 and 2; page 28), but use Buttonhole stitch at the corner and along the straight edges to neaten.

Join in a thread at B. Pull the threads together with Coral stitches (see page 28, Fig 2 for Coral stitch). Sew the thread out at C.

Sew in new threads as shown and work Coral stitches at the inter-sections, but crossing the threads at A without joining them. Cross the threads at the corner and sew them out at C. Repeat, from B, on the other side.

When all the threads are in pos-ition, work Spider Filling Wheels and Clover Leaves, alternating them on the groups of threads at the points A (Fig 2).

Spider Filling Wheels
Join the thread to the centre at A, securing the group of threads with a Coral stitch. Needle-weave the thread round the centre, over and under, 6 or 7 times. As there are an even number of threads, it will be necessary to cross 2 threads once on each round to keep the weaving even. Finish off with a few stitches in the centre of the Wheel. (Refer to page 17, Fig 5, for Spider Filling.)

Clover Leaves
Secure the weaving thread to the centre at A. Divide the threads so that there are 3 threads at the top and bottom, and 4 threads to the left and right (see Fig 3). Begin weaving from the centre, under and over the group of three threads, to the top of the leaf.

Work a Coral stitch at the top to secure the thread, then bring it back to the centre across the woven leaf shape. Work the side 4 threads in the same way, over and under, but only to about three-quarters of the way along, then weave on the central 2 threads only to the tip of the leaf shape.

Corner flower
This is a much larger hole; in order to keep the work even, baste the fabric to a piece of brown wrapping paper, or draughtsman's tracing linen. Each petal has 7 threads. Attach the thread to the centre, making sure the 'spokes' are evenly spaced.

Weave under and over 7 threads until halfway, then over the central 5 for a further quarter of the way round, then over the central threads to the top.

Secure the thread, and bring it back to the centre across the petal.

Work all the petals in the same way (see detail). Finish off the thread in the centre.

Finishing
Remove the fabric from the paper by unpicking the basting threads. Press the work on the wrong side over a soft, padded surface.

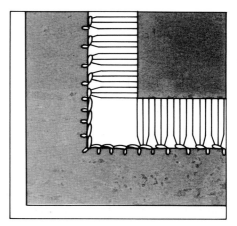

Fig 1 *Preparing the corner with Hemstitching and Buttonhole stitching*

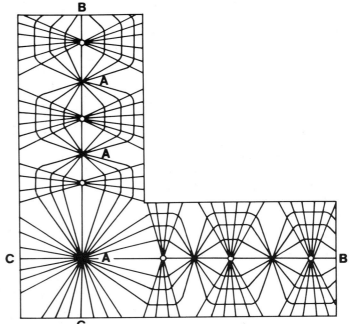

Fig 2 *Working diagram for the cloth corner and edge*

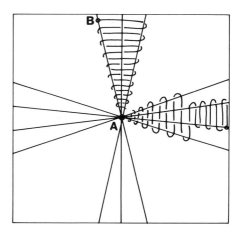

Fig 3 *Working diagram for the Clover Leaves*

Reticella Lace

Most forms of cutwork are associated with Italy and Reticella is the name given to the lace, worked on a framework of cut and drawn threads. The picture of a Reticella strip on page 8 shows the finest of the work that could be achieved in the sixteenth century. The intricate designs were numerous.

Threads are removed leaving square or rectangular holes, held together with just a few of the original warp and weft threads. These areas are filled with geometric patterns of Buttonhole stitched bars, in various formations. The strip inserted into the lampshade is an

Lampshade with a strip of antique Reticella work inserted

antique sampler, worked on very fine linen. Twelve different geometric constructions appear on the sampler, and one section has been abstracted as a sample rectangle for you to work. This pattern can be enlarged or reduced to suit its use. Crochet cotton or wool could be used to make a cushion cover or very fine thread for a pincushion motif.

Materials required

Firm, evenweave fabric, cotton, linen, or linen-type

Embroidery threads of the same (or contrasting) colour, slightly thicker than threads withdrawn from the fabric

Preparation for working

The detail and the pattern (Fig 1) are life-size. Work your sample to this size also. Mark the area on the fabric with running stitches, following the weft and warp threads. Count threads to find the centre of the fabric. Leaving 4 threads of the warp and 4 threads of the weft in a cross at the centre of the fabric, cut away and withdraw the other threads.

Working the design

Buttonhole-stitch round the area on all four sides.

Needle-weave the centre threads where they cross, to strengthen the piece (Fig 2).

Trace the design from Fig 1 onto a piece of firm, brown wrapping paper, or draughtsman's tracing linen.

Place the fabric on the traced pattern, matching the edges and the crossed threads at the centre. Baste all round, and also along the fabric bars.

Working threads are attached to the solid fabric areas only. The Buttonhole-stitched bars are worked on the surface of the paper (as for the Richelieu technique page 17).

Set a diagonal thread from A to B, (Fig 1) return from B to A, then back through B to the centre of the cross. Three threads have now been laid.

Buttonhole-stitch from B to the first curved line of the design. Drop the thread out to the sides 3 times (as in the Richelieu technique, page 17, Fig 2). Buttonhole-stitch the curved bar (Fig 4).

Buttonhole-stitch to C, and drop out the thread for the diagonal to D, back to E, and back to D again. Buttonhole-stitch from D to the curved bar, and repeat the working down to C.

Detail of the Reticella strip, showing one section

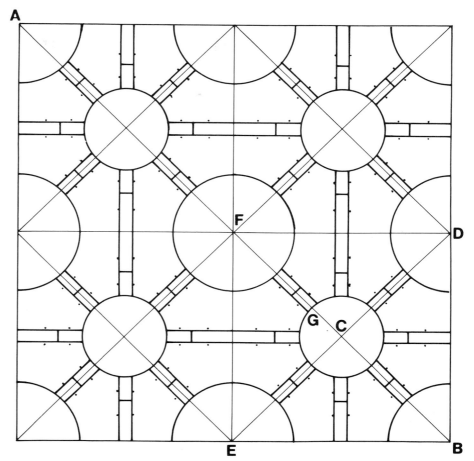

Fig 1 *Trace this life-sized pattern onto linen or firm paper*

Take the thread from C to E and repeat the Buttonhole-stitching back to C.

Take the thread to F and repeat the Buttonhole-stitching down to G.

Take the thread round the centre 3 times, working through the bar threads, and back to G. Buttonhole-stitch this ring, dropping out the thread for the Bullion picot bars which join the curves, and to H, I, J and K (Fig 5). These are joined together with a thread as they are worked on the line marked and the dots indicate picots (Fig 3).

This works one quarter of the design.

Start the next section at A on the opposite side. When this is completed, lay another set of diagonal stitches to work the remaining two sections.

Finishing

Remove the completed Reticella piece from the paper and press on the wrong side over a soft, padded surface.

If you are working a strip of repeats of the rectangle, draw and cut all the threads first, Buttonhole-stitch round all the edges of the rectangles and needle-weave the bars, then baste the whole piece to paper, as described.

Fig 2 *Needle-weave the fabric threads where they cross*
Fig 3 *One-quarter section of the Fig 1 pattern*
Fig 4 *Buttonhole-stitch each curved bar as it is reached in working*
Fig 5 *Work Bullion picots on bars, marked as dots on the pattern (Fig 1) and the quarter-section (Fig 3). Take the needle back into the looped edge of the last Buttonhole stitch, twist the working thread 6 times round the body of the needle, then pull through. To set the picot, make the next Buttonhole stitch close up to the last worked*

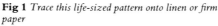

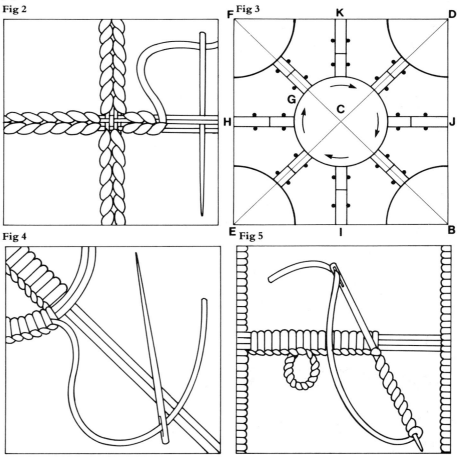

CHAPTER THREE

NEEDLE LACE

By the seventeenth century, the link with the woven fabric was broken and needle lace became a fabric in its own right. Again, Italy had taken the initiative and *Punto in Aria* (stitches in the air) was developed, the phrase expressing the idea that stitching could be done without it being permanently attached to fabric.

Fashion changed and softer, more pliable laces were in demand. Dress fabrics were richly coloured which allowed lace to be displayed against them to advantage and lace was used lavishly on both women's and men's clothes, as well as furnishings.

The first pattern books produced for needle lace were for stitches to be worked over parchment. Italian Reticella was different to that made in Flanders and, although still geometric, it acquired a more flowing design, depicting flowers, animals and figures, all within the confines of the square-cut grid. The techniques for building peaks and loops freely on the edges of cutwork was also an Italian idea and, on the fashionable ruff, the decorative edge was most attractive.

Needle laces were expensive and treasured and, in society, lace was an emblem of prestige. Venetian laces were greatly in demand and most countries in Europe were importing them. This caused some countries to experience economic problems and France, in particular, relied heavily on the importation of luxury goods and lace was an important one. The French Government decided to support its own lacemaking industry and invited Venetian and Flemish lacemakers to France to help and advise. The production of Point de France was soon under way in established lacemaking centres and the lace was an almost immediate success, especially with the court of Louis XIV. A more pliable lace was required for the gathered cravats and falling cuffs. Women's dresses had full, lace flounces and tall, lace headdresses were all the rage. By 1700, Point de France was the most sought-after lace in Europe.

The eighteenth century was, however, the finest period for lace. The techniques were developed and the linen thread, produced in Flanders, was of high quality and extremely fine. Silk was also beginning to be used but it was not so popular with the needle lacemakers, being difficult to work, but the resulting lace was extremely soft and delicate.

Bobbin lace, which has its origins in weaving, was beginning to be regarded as an important fabric in its own right. These two types, needle lace and bobbin lace, have run alongside each other throughout the history of lace and, at various times, one would outpace the other in fashion. The two techniques came together in Tape Lace which, again, was started in Italy.

Designing and pricking lace patterns at Arenys de Mar, Spain

The Geometric form

The geometric design produced by the Reticella technique could also be worked without the linen ground. Instead of linen warp and weft threads, threads were laid on paper or cardboard and then the same stitches as were used for Reticella work were worked over them.

British needlewomen of the nineteenth century took to the craft and, as the thread used was thicker than that used for needle lacemaking, the resulting lace was hardwearing and eminently suitable for furnishings and house linens.

The tablecloth in the picture is a typical Victorian 'lace patchwork'. There are examples of different kinds of lace within it, including the geo- metric form of design.

A Cross motif and Butterfly (see details) have been abstracted for you to work. Both patterns can be used as inserts on garments or on household linens. It is recommended that the Cross motif be worked first.

Materials required

Thin card, or draughtsman's tracing linen
Linen, or cotton thread (Madeira No 30)
Strong sewing thread

CROSS MOTIF

Preparing to work

Trace the design (Fig 1) onto thin card. Pierce pinholes in the card where the design lines touch the outline. Pierce holes where the lines meet each other.

Thread a needle with doubled sewing thread and knot the ends.

Following the arrows on the lines in the bottom right quarter of the design (Fig 1), lay the thread along the lines, working from pinhole to pinhole. Work a Cross stitch where marked at intersections in Fig 1.

Now lay threads round the outline of the design, taking the thread through the ends of the threads already laid. Work from A to A, round the design, 3 times. Now take the thread from A to B, through the centre C, 3 times, finishing at B.

Working the design

To reduce bulk, the diagonal laid threads are tightly whipped, but the branch lines are Buttonhole-stitched.

From B, whip the laid threads down to D, working the curved bars with picots in Buttonhole stitch (see small circles on the curved lines in Fig

Various types of lace are used in this beautiful Victorian tablecloth

Detail of the Cross motif from the Victorian tablecloth

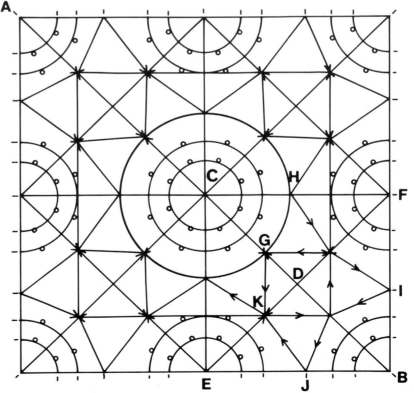

Fig 1 *Trace this diagram for the Cross motif, and refer to it during working*

1). At D, take the thread to E, across to F and back to E. Work E to D by whipping, working curved bars as before. Take the thread from D to F and work F to D.

Whip from D to G and, at this point, take the thread through the Cross stitches, and back to G 3 times.

Take the thread out to the points of the triangles, H, I, J, K, once.

These triangles are worked in Corded Buttonhole stitch, over a laid thread (see Fig 2). The stitch is always worked from left to right.

Work from the base line over the 3 laid threads, decreasing 1 stitch on each row to the point.

At the completion of the triangle, take the thread across the back of the work to start the next triangle.

Work anti-clockwise until all the triangles are completed, back to G. Finish the thread G to C.

Complete the other three sections of the motif in the same way. Use as long a thread as you can cope with so that there are as few ends as possible. Begin and finish threads by weaving ends into the Buttonhole-stitched bars.

Finishing
When the work is completed, cut the threads that hold the work to the card and carefully lift off the lace. It can now be inserted into a tablecloth or a traycloth, or even into a fabric lampshade.

Inserting lace motifs
Baste the motif to the right side of fabric, matching the grain lines. Work Buttonhole stitches round the piece of lace. Cut the fabric away behind the lace.

Several motifs can be joined together by Buttonholing each to the next. Insert the strip of joined motifs in the same way as described for a single motif.

Lace in colour
Butterflies, such as the motif opposite, make excellent design motifs for coloured lace. The wings can be divided into areas of different stitches and the 'eyes' on the wings can be achieved with Buttonhole Rings. Although motifs look fresh and attractive in white or ecru, an effective butterfly can be achieved by using coloured threads. Use random-coloured thread or work the motif in realistic colours. Try working an Orange Tip Butterfly with white fillings, an orange triangle at the tip of the upper wing and a grey body. A Red Admiral can be worked in black, white and red thread. For displaying butterflies, Buttonhole-stitch fine wire round the outer edge, after the work is completed.

Detail from the centre area of the Victorian tablecloth showing the Butterfly motif

BUTTERFLY MOTIF

This is worked in the same way as the Cross motif but it is advisable to work the Cross first so that the principles are understood.

Trace the butterfly from Fig 3 and baste the tracing to thin card. Work the laid threads with doubled sewing thread as for the Cross motif, with Cross stitches at intersections.

Work Buttonhole-stitched bars for the lower body. Work the head with Corded Buttonhole stitch (Fig 2) and then work Buttonhole-stitched bars on either side.

Lay 3 threads from B to C and from B to D, returning to C. Whip from C to E, setting in the other diagonals and bars as they are reached. (There are several radiating bars and care is needed to keep the centres neat.)

At E, work the inner circle and work Buttonhole stitch round it.

Continue to whip to F, then set in the outer circle threads.

Work the triangular areas as for the Cross motif, using Corded Buttonhole stitch. Work triangles in an anti-clockwise direction, back to F:

Whip to B and whip and Buttonhole-stitch to D.

Finish off the thread end.

Start the lower wing by setting the diagonal G to H, and work as the upper wing from G.

Work the other wings in the same way.

Finishing

Remove the lace from the card carefully, cutting the threads that hold the work to the card. The butterfly motif can be inserted into fabric using the same technique as for the Cross motif.

After inserting the motif, work the antennae in Stem stitch or Satin stitch on the surface of the fabric.

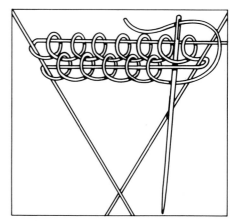

Fig 2 *Corded Buttonhole stitch is always worked from left to right over a laid thread*

Fig 3 *Trace the Butterfly for a pattern, then refer to it during working*

Teneriffe Wheels or Suns

At some time in the seventeenth century, the techniques for making Sol lace changed. The background fabric was abandoned and the suns or wheels were worked freely over a piece of stiff linen. Running stitches were worked in a circle and threads laid across the centre, the number of threads varying with the design. Needle-weaving and Coral stitch were used to form the intricate patterns and, when the work was finished, the running threads were cut to release the lace.

This technique travelled with the Spaniards to South America and Mexico and the skills passed to the local people. The thread they used was fine, often of silk, and the lace they produced was very delicate. It was made in Bolivia, Brazil, Peru and Paraguay and became known as *Nanduti* (web). Nanduti lace was used for church vestments, and on dress, and was soon exported to Europe.

The people of Teneriffe also learned how to make Nanduti lace but they adapted the technique. Instead of using linen and running threads, they used a small, round, leather-topped 'pincushion', which could be held in the palm of the hand. Pins were inserted round the 'pincushion' and the threads wound

Nineteenth-century handkerchief trimmed with South American Nanduti lace

Detail from the handkerchief

around them. Once the wheel of lace was completed the pins were removed and the lace released.

Lacemaking by this method is still used in Teneriffe but it is a cottage industry for the tourist market and the work produced does not compare to that of the nineteenth century when the handkerchief in the picture was produced. The lace on the handkerchief, probably made in South America, is of a very fine thread.

A wheel motif had been abstracted for you to work (see detail).

Small Teneriffe wheels can be inserted, or used as appliqué motifs, for fashion clothes and accessories, household linens, furnishings etc. The motif here would be pretty worked for the corner of a handkerchief. Worked in coarser threads, perhaps to a diameter of 20cm (8in), the wheel could be used to make a window 'snowflake', stitched to a metal ring.

Materials required
Thin card
Non-stretch threads (cotton, linen, silk)
Blunt-tipped needle
Piece of polystyrene tile
Pins with large heads

Preparation
The method of working described is similar to that used by the natives of Teneriffe but, if you prefer, work the design over a piece of stiff fabric or draughtsman's tracing linen. Pierce pinholes on the circle, and work running threads round twice so that every hole on the perimeter is filled and then lay the 'spokes' of the wheel under the running stitches.

Alternatively, draw a circle to the size of wheel desired. Measure and mark the centre of the circle. Using pencil compasses, mark the edge of the circle into segments. There should be an even number of divisions, and the number, doubled, be divisible by 12 (ie 60, 72, 84, 96, 108 etc). The design given here has 180 threads laid, thus 90 marks are made round the circle. Place the card on the tile and push a pin into each of the marks. Push a pin into the middle of the circle. Tie the thread end round the pin. Take the thread round the circle of pins, following the route indicated in Fig 1. Finish at the centre.

Working the design
Follow the quarter-section of the wheel (Fig 2). Using the same thread, weave round the centre, over 2 threads, under 2, working 5 or 6 rounds. Finish the thread end off. Now work at the outer edge of the wheel.

1st row Work Coral stitches (see page 28, Fig 2) over every 2 threads.

2nd row Alternating the spacing, work Coral stitches over every 2 threads.

Working at the centre again, work Coral stitches over 2 threads at the point which will be the bottom of the petals (Fig 2), dropping down on every 2 Coral stitches to group 12

threads together with a Coral stitch. Keep the tension even.

Working the petals
Work the 15 petals of the design by needle-weaving groups of twelve threads (Fig 2). About half-way up the petal, decrease the width by 1 thread on each side but continue weaving to the tip.

Work a Coral stitch at the tip and take the thread down at the back of the work to weave the next petal.

When all the petals have been worked, work Coral stitches over the petals, each stitch on a single thread, to outline the flower.

At the end of the round, fasten the thread end into the first Coral stitch.

Remove the pins and release the lace.

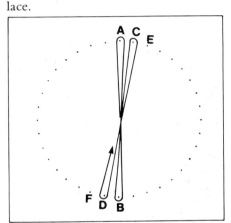

Fig 1 *Take threads round the pins as shown, crossing the threads in the middle of the circle*

Fig 2 *A quarter-section of the Teneriffe wheel pattern*

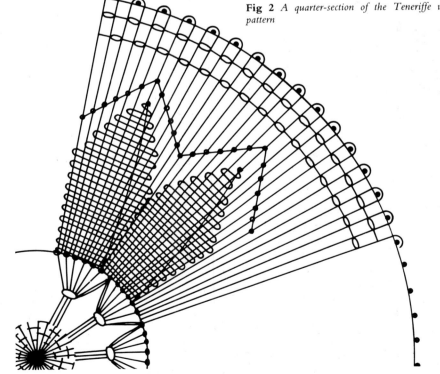

Floral Needle Lace

Once the technique of needle lace-making was fully developed there were very few limitations in design. A thread could be made to travel the same route as a drawn line, and shapes could filled with dense or open stitches to create textures. The motifs could be joined with bars, or by an open, needle-made net, and there was no difficulty in starting or ending threads. Needle lace became as free as any other form of free-style embroidery.

Needle lace is made in the same way today as in the seventeenth century and only the threads have changed – very fine threads are no longer available.

BUTTERFLIES ON TOWELS

These butterfly motifs are caught to the towelling and, made of a washable cotton thread, they will last through many launderings. Fig 1 is a life-size pattern.

Materials required
Architect's or draughtsman's tracing linen (or used coloured paper with self-adhesive film applied to one side)
Thread: Choose from cotton, linen or silk lacemaking threads; stranded embroidery cotton; Coton à Broder
Fabric for backing
Basting thread
Blunt-tipped needle
Sewing needles, (sharps)
Sharp, pointed embroidery scissors

Preparation
Trace the butterfly design from Fig 1. Trace the design onto architect's linen or onto coloured paper. If you are using coloured paper, apply plastic self-adhesive film to the top side.

Prick holes at 2mm (1/16in) intervals along all the design lines, using a fine needle. Baste the pricked pattern to doubled fabric (firm cotton or linen).

Couch a double strand of the working thread round the design, (called the 'trace thread'), using soft basting cotton for couching, and working the stitches through the doubled thickness of fabric. (Make sure that the couched thread is long enough to go all round the design. It may not matter if the basting thread is long enough because this can be fastened off and rejoined on the wrong side of the work.) Begin and end at the antennae.

Fig 2 shows the technique for couching threads along design lines.

Working the design
Butterfly body
Work the body in Corded Buttonhole stitch (page 39, Fig 2). Work over the couched thread from left to right.

Start and finish by making a few stitches over the couched edging and always make sure that there is sufficient thread to finish a row. A thread can be started in the middle of a row.

Work from the tail tip to the head. Make the loops of even size – they must be neither too loose nor too tight, and your tension will improve with practice. At the end of the row, take the needle under and over the edge and return the needle to the left.

Work the next row through the loops of the previous row and over the laid thread. When the space is filled, whip the thread end to the couched threads. Fasten off the thread end.

Butterfly motifs on soft towelling

The Butterfly motif, just over life-size. The pattern is below

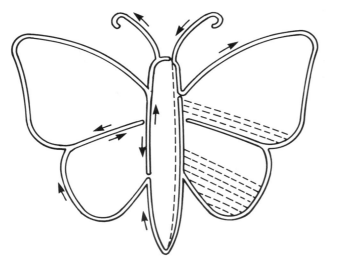

Fig 1 *Trace-off pattern for the Butterfly motif*

Wings

Work the wings in open fillings. Many fillings are worked in rows without laid threads so, to travel from left to right, turn the work and make one row with the needle towards you and the next row with the needle away from you.

Work the lower wing in Double Brussels stitch (Fig 3a and b) and the upper wing in Treble Brussels stitch (see caption, Fig 3b).

There are many variations on Brussels stitch made by spacing loops and working various numbers of Buttonhole stitches in the spaces – such as 4, 1, 1, 4 or 3, 2, 2, 3 – and so on.

When all the surface work is complete, the outlining threads of the design are made bolder by Buttonhole-stitching 4 threads on the same route as the trace thread, arranging the knots on the outside edge. In some parts, take 2 threads up and back to keep the continuity of the edge. Sometimes it will be necessary to Buttonhole-stitch towards you, and sometimes away from you, to keep the edge continuous.

If new thread is required, join it with a few stitches to the original trace thread.

Finishing

Separate the two layers of fabric and cut the basting threads. While the lace is still attached to the paper, remove the basting threads holding the couching threads – they can be seen on the back of the pattern. Remove the lace from the paper. The procedure described here is the basis of all the needlelace patterns in this chapter.

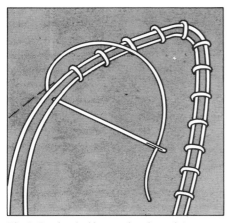

Fig 2 *Couch a double trace thread round the pattern lines, using soft basting thread for couching. Work stitches through the double thickness of fabric*

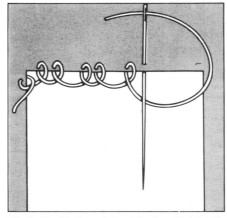

Fig 3a *Double Buttonhole stitch, also called Double Brussels stitch: 1st row, work Buttonhole stitches in groups of two to the end of the row with the needle towards the body*

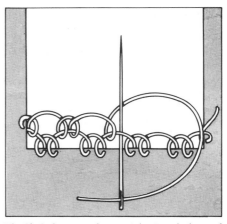

Fig 3b *2nd row, work two stitches into the loops of the previous row, needle away from the body. Treble Brussels stitch has 3 stitches instead of two; Single Brussels stitch has 1 stitch*

Point de Gaze

The Belgian lace industry of the seventeenth century was firmly established but, sadly, very few pieces of lace from this period have survived. By far the most common lace to be found today is Point de Gaze. This was developed in the mid-nineteenth century from the old Flemish needle point laces to fill a fashion demand for a light, airy lace.

It had flower motifs and the Victorians loved flower designs – the rose was their favourite, and it appeared in every form from buds to full-blown flowers. Point de Gaze became very popular and was extensively used for dress flounces, collars, wedding veils, shawls, handkerchiefs and for accessories such as parasols and fans.

Motifs were held together by a very light, open-looped net, made of an extremely fine thread. Shading, such as on rose petals, was very naturalistic and achieved with close, or open, Buttonhole stitches. The motifs were outlined with light Buttonholing, and the lace acquired its name from its gauzy appearance.

By the 1870s, the rose motifs had been given extra petals, and sometimes as many as three layers of petals were made separately and stitched to the ground lace, giving the lace an extra dimension.

Large areas of lace, such as for a shawl, were made in pieces and afterwards joined, joins being concealed with sprigs or sprays of flowers. This method of working enabled several workers to work on the same piece of lace – speed of execution was essential to meet the demand. Large Point de Gaze shawls were a popular accessory and had considerable appeal for fashion-conscious Victorian ladies.

Point de Gaze was made up to the end of the nineteenth century and then pieces began to be mixed with Duchess bobbin lace, also made in Brussels, such as the cuff in the picture, which has a medallion of needle lace set in bobbin lace flowers. The rose has the extra petals but there is no doubt that the work at the end of the century was nowhere near as fine as that of the earlier years.

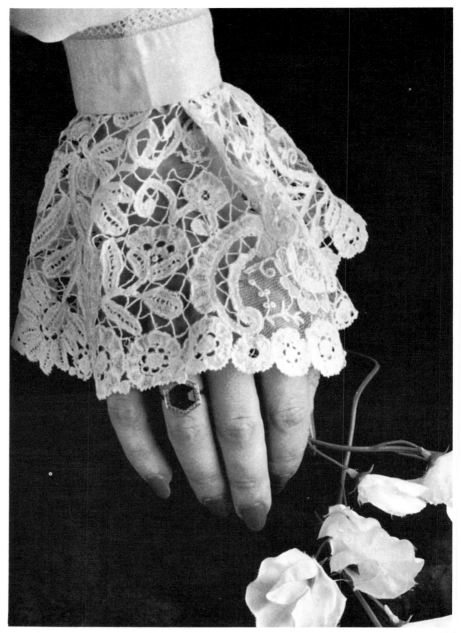

A deep, Point de Gaze lace cuff, with needlelace and bobbin lace flowers

The flower has been abstracted for you to work and the motif would be beautiful for lingerie or for personal accessories.

The motif pattern provided is larger than the original because modern threads are not fine enough to work a flower of the original size.

OPEN ROSE

Materials requried

Architects or draughtsman's tracing linen or coloured paper with self-adhesive film on one side
Firm fabric for mounting the pattern
Thread: Choose from Gütermans pure silk 100/3; DMC Retours D'Alsace 30; Madeira No 50

Stranded embroidery cotton (1 strand used)

Preparation

Trace the design from Fig 1 onto tracing linen or coloured paper. Prick holes 2mm (1/16in) apart on all the design lines. Baste the pricked pattern to doubled fabric.

Couch 2 threads on all design lines in a continuous line, including leaves, tendrils etc (see page 43, Fig 2 for the technique for couching). Work small basting stitches on the background dots, (see pattern) to support the ground stitches which are worked later.

Working the design

Work Corded Buttonhole stitch (page 39, Fig 2) on the lower petals, central petal, small leaves and half of the large leaves, working in the directions indicated by the pattern.

Work Twisted Buttonhole stitch (page 25, Figs 2a and 2b) in the upper petals down to the line marked on the pattern, in the upper half of the lower petals and in the other half of the leaves.

Work a Spider Filling (page 17, Fig 5) in the flower centre.

Work Twisted Buttonhole stitch in the net area between the flowers, attaching it to the leaves, tendrils and stalks. Work the stitch larger than that in the flower petals by taking the working thread through the small basting stitches before making the Buttonhole stitch. This keeps the net evenly-sized.

Make Buttonhole Rings (Fig 2) and attach them to the flower centres. Buttonhole-stitch over 2 threads all round the design, and on all the veins and petal separating lines. Buttonhole stitch on both sides of stalks and tendrils.

Release the lace from the fabric (see page 43 for procedure).

Detail from the cuff, showing the abstracted flower motif

Finishing

To attach the lace to fabric, catch the edges down very lightly. Attach the inner edge of the design with Back stitches or Buttonhole stitches. Cut away the fabric behind the net very carefully. An extra central petal can be made if desired and attached. Make several Buttonhole Rings and attach them to the background material.

Fig 1 *Trace-off pattern for the Point de Gaze motif*

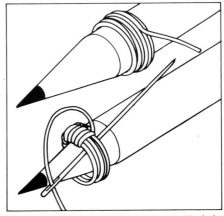

Fig 2 *Buttonhole Ring or Couronne: Wind the thread around the pencil point 8–10 times, then work 3 or 4 Buttonhole stitches over the threads to secure. Slip the loops from the pencil and work Buttonhole stitches all round to complete the Ring. Attach Rings with the thread end*

FLOWER COLLAR

This pretty flower collar is designed to be fitted around a round or boat-shaped neckline but it can also be used on bare-shouldered dresses or blouses as an unusual and distinctive form of 'jewellery'. The original collar was worked in coloured threads (see the illustration on the back cover), but it would look equally pretty worked in white, cream or ecru thread or, for a dramatic accessory, in black thread. Small pearl beads could be attached for additional interest.

Materials required

Architect's or draughtsman's tracing linen (or use coloured paper with self-adhesive film applied to one side)
Fabric for backing
Basting thread
Thread: Gütermans pure silk 100/3 spools, 1 each of pale pink, dark pink, fawn, green (or use the same number of balls in a single colour)
Stranded embroidery cotton (1 strand used)

Preparation

Trace the collar motifs from Fig 1 and Fig 2. The large rose fits to the ends of the main collar, to hang at the front (see picture).

Reverse the tracing and re-trace, matching the pattern, to achieve a pattern for the whole collar. Transfer the designs to the tracing linen or paper. Needle-prick all the design lines, 2mm (¹⁄₁₆in) apart. Baste the pricked design to doubled fabric.

Couch all the design lines with doubled trace threads. If you are working in coloured threads, couch the flower shapes in pink thread and the leaves in green thread. Couch a pink thread in a figure-of-eight round the rings of the flower centres.

Work small basting stitches on the pattern dots, to support the ground stitches which are worked later.

Working the design

Work Corded Buttonhole stitch in the centre petals and on the turned-up edges of the flowers, half of each leaf, and all the stalks.

Work Corded Buttonhole stitch, with holes, in the petals that are attached afterwards (refer to Fig 5 on page 53).

Work Pea stitch (see Fig 3) in the remainder of the flower petals and work Twisted Buttonhole stitch (page 25, Figs 2a and 2b) in the other half of the leaves.

Make Buttonhole-stitched bars to join the motifs as indicated (see pattern, Fig 1), carrying the thread along by whipping it over the trace thread to the next bar position.

Work Open Twisted Buttonhole stitch (Figs 4a and 4b) for the background (if you are working in colour, use fawn thread), using the basted threads as support to keep the net even.

Finish the collar edges with Buttonhole stitches worked over two laid threads all round the design, matching colour changes where they occur.

Work the veins, inner petal marking and stems in the same way.

Make Buttonhole Rings (page 45, Fig 2), and attach them to the flower centres, making sure that they are joined to each other. Whip the bars that support the rings.

Finishing

Release the lace following the procedures described on page 43.

Note The collar (see picture) can be worked without the central linking flower motif and worn in a similar way to a 'Peter Pan' collar.

The flower collar and the extra, large rose motif, illustrated in colour on the back book cover

Fig 1 *Trace-off pattern for the Point de Gaze flowers. Join the two sections on the design lines.*

Fig 2 *The large rose motif which hangs at the front (see back cover). Trace the half given here, reverse the tracing and re-trace for the complete pattern*

Fig 4a *Open Twisted Buttonhole stitch: Work from left to right, needle towards the body*

Fig 3 *Pea stitch: On the 1st row, work close Buttonhole stitches left to right. On the 2nd row, work 2 and miss 2. On the 3rd row, work 3 stitches into the large loop and 1 stitch in the small loop. Repeat 2nd row*

Fig 4b *On the second row, work stitches onto the loops of the previous row, needle away from the body*

47

GALLEON IN LACE

Needle lace can also be worked to make a dimensional picture. This Galleon is made in separate pieces and assembled on a fabric ground. All the procedures and stitches can be found in the needle made lace chapter on the previous pages.

Materials required

Finished dimensions: 22.5×17.5cm (9×7in)

Architect's or draughtsman's tracing linen (or coloured paper with self-adhesive film applied to one side)

Backing fabric

Fabric for mounting the picture

Basting thread

Sewing thread, matched to the lace thread colour: Choose from DMC Retours d'Alsace 30; Brok 36; Madeira No 30; Coats Chain-Mercer Crochet cotton No 60

Stranded embroidery cotton (1 thread used)

Preparation

Trace the various parts of the Galleon from the life-size patterns on page 50. Transfer the patterns to the tracing linen or prepared paper. Needle-prick all the design lines, 2mm (¹⁄₁₆in) apart.

Couch doubled-thread trace threads over all the design lines. Baste the pattern to doubled fabric.

Working the design

Hull Work areas of open stitches alternating with Corded Buttonhole stitch (page 39) with the dividing lines worked in Buttonhole stitch over 4 laid threads.

Work the windows in Pea stitch (page 47), outlined in Buttonhole stitch over 2 laid threads. Work Buttonhole Rings (see Fig 2, page 45) for the portholes.

Waves Work the waves in stitches of your choice, and outline them with Buttonhole stitch over 2 laid threads. (Note: you will need 12 of the scrolled wave shapes altogether to complete the design.)

Masts Work the masts in loosely-worked Corded Buttonhole stitch and outline them in Buttonhole stitch

Detail of the sails, rigging and flags
Detail of the hull and waves

Trace-off patterns for working parts of the Galleon are on page 50

Trace these patterns to work the Galleon in Lace picture. Trace the waves 3 times for 12 waves over 4 laid threads. Work the masts at the same time as the sails.

Sails Work these in Open Corded Buttonhole stitch (the broken lines indicate the direction of working). On the broken lines, work 1 row of Twisted Buttonhole stitch, missing alternate loops to make a row of holes. Continue with the Corded Buttonhole stitch, making 2 stitches into each Twisted Buttonhole stitch.

Work the tops of the sails in Buttonhole stitch over 6 laid threads, but work plain Buttonhole stitch round the edges of the sails so that they do not have a heavy edge.

Flags Work these in any filling stitch to your choice.

Rigging Work Buttonhole stitch closely over the couched threads, working bars where indicated on the pattern. Buttonhole-stitch the bars.

Work 5 rigging strands for the topsails, a longer rigging for the foresail and 4 long rigging strands for the lower sails.

Finishing
Remove the lace from the pattern.

Following the picture, place the hull on the background fabric. Pin in position along the bottom edge and at the ends. The top edge is left free of the background fabric making a 'pocket', so that dimensional effect is achieved.

Arrange the waves and pin in position. Position the tall mast in the centre, the bottom end inside the hull of the galleon. The remaining masts are positioned at each side. Attach the masts to the background with a few stitches, using sewing thread and making stitches as unobtrusive as possible. Stitch down the hull and waves in the same way.

Attach the rigging so that some lies to the back of the galleon, within the 'pocket' of the hull, and some to the front over the hull, where they can be attached to the edge realistically.

A dimensional picture such as this should be mounted on heavy card, the edges of the fabric laced at the back, the picture then framed in a box frame.

Point de Venise

This beautiful Venetian needle lace has the bold, stylised flowers and curling stems and leaves of the Baroque period. With smooth, raised areas, heavily ornamented edges and a rich, sculptured appearance, it resembles carved ivory.

Point de Venise was made in different sizes, from the Gros Point which was used for dress, furnishings, and altar frontals, to the smallest and finest Point de Neige, said to resemble snow flakes with its myriads of tiny, raised stars and rings.

Venetian needle laces were fashionable throughout the seventeenth and eighteenth centuries. They suited the formal court dress and were imported by almost every European country.

Point de Venise was very expensive and it is recorded that a length intended for cuffs cost 32 shillings in 1668, which was more than most people earned in a year. Each piece of lace was treasured, and altered as fashion changed. It is rare today to find a piece of eighteenth-century lace that has not been cut and re-shaped.

Point de Venise has a distinctive design and method of working. The motifs are worked in Corded Buttonhole stitch with a few areas of the more open fillings. These are embellished with raised, padded Buttonhole-stitched surrounds, some padded with a hundred extra threads. These areas then have a further edge of picots and worked bars, to give added dimension and the whole is joined with richly ornamented bars.

The detail below shows the Venetian point motifs which have been abstracted to make the 'soft jewellery' on pages 52–53. Before attempting the jewellery, try making a strip of Point de Venise edging, which can be worked along the edge of a handkerchief or along the edges of a fabric collar (see Figs 1–3 pages 52–53).

POINT DE VENISE EDGING

Materials required
A handkerchief with a rolled edge, or a fabric edge with a turned, double narrow hem
Thread: Choose from Gütermans pure silk; linen lacemaking threads; sewing thread

Preparation for working
Attach the thread end to the fabric edge with a few neat stitches.

Working the design
Fig 2 shows the first and second row of the edging being worked.

Make a loop by taking the thread a short distance away to the right and take a stitch in the fabric edge. Take

Venetian Lace with the flowers, stems and leaves which are typical of the Baroque period

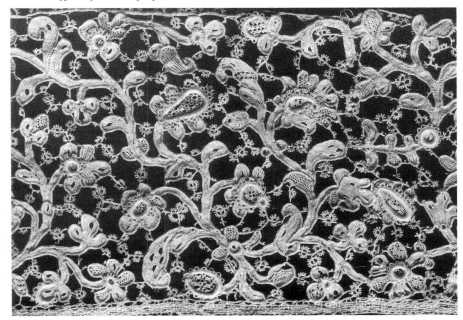

the needle back to the point where it came through and take another stitch.

This makes a 2-thread loop. Work the 2-thread loop again to make a 4-thread loop. The thread is at the left hand side. Work close Buttonhole stitch along the loop until the right hand end of the loop is reached.

Make a second 4-thread loop and Buttonhole-stitch closely, as before, but make a picot in the centre of the loop (Fig 3). Continue Buttonhole stitching to the end.

Make a third 4-thread loop and begin Buttonhole-stitching, but at the half-way point take the thread back to the centre of the first loop, and catch it to the Buttonhole stitches (Fig 2).

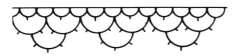

Fig 1 *Point de Venise edging, showing 3 rows worked*

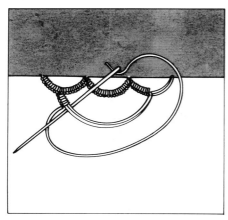

Fig 2 *Working the loops for Point de Venise edging, row 2 started from the 3rd loop of row 1*

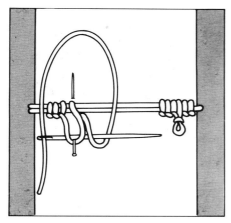

Fig 3 *Loop picot: Buttonhole-stitch to the position of the picot, and insert a pin. Place the working thread under the head of the pin, from left to right, over the bar, and out beneath it. Work a Buttonhole stitch over the loop and pull up tightly to secure. Continue with Buttonhole stitching*

Work this branching thread twice more between the third loop and the first, so that there are 3 threads, and then Buttonhole-stitch these threads. Repeat this movement for the loops on the third row (Fig 1). Continue until the lace is the length required.

NECKLACE AND EARRINGS

Materials required
Architect's or draughtsman's tracing linen
Fabric for backing
Stranded embroidery cotton (use 1 thread for couching)
Thread: 6 spools of Gütermans pure silk 100/3
Pearl beads
Pearl stud earrings
Gilt chain

Preparation for working
Trace all the motifs and two extra flowers from Fig 4 onto tracing linen.

Prick along all the design lines using a needle, pricking holes 2mm (1/16in) apart. Baste the tracing to doubled fabric.

Couch a doubled thread round each motif (see page 43, Fig 2 for the method of couching).

Working the design
Work Corded Buttonhole stitch, with a hole in the centre (Fig 5) in the petals marked. Work the stitch in the direction of the hole as indicated by the dotted lines on the pattern. Work the Twisted Buttonhole stitch (page 25, Figs 2a and 2b) in the other flower petals and in the side motifs. Work the variation of the filling from Fig 6 in the centre of the main motif.

Work a closely-worked Buttonhole-stitched edge round each motif over 6 laid threads. Work Buttonhole Rings (Couronnes) with picots (Fig 2, page 45), and attach to the flower centre. Work the large, oval centres by Buttonhole-stitching over 12 laid threads and working a picot bar at the same time.

Work the large oval of the centre motif by laying in threads gradually to give a tapered effect. Start with 4 threads at the point and, adding 3 threads at a time, increase to 34 threads. (Short lengths of thread only are required).

Whip these threads to the trace thread, decreasing them again to 4 at that point. Buttonhole-stitch these threads closely and evenly, while making a Point de Venise edging from the Buttonhole stitching (Refer to the instructions for Figs 2 and 3).

Take care that the loops are even and do not catch the work below.

Make a further 5 Buttonhole Rings and attach them to the filling in the centre motif and to the tips of the side motifs. Sew pearl beads into the centres of the rings.

Release the lace from the fabric.

Finishing
Attach the lace necklace to the ends of the gilt chain with a few stitches. Push the earring studs through the centres of the lace flowers.

Fig 4 *Trace-off patterns for the necklace motifs and flower earrings*

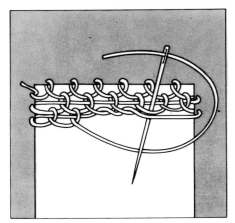

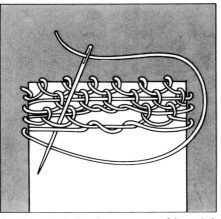

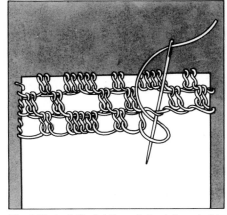

Fig 5 *Corded Buttonhole stitch with holes, also called Corded Brussels stitch: Decide on the length of the hole. On the return row, right to left, whip the thread through the loops of the previous row for the*

length required. On the return row of Buttonhole stitch, miss the whipped loops and continue. Bring the thread back to the left and whip two or three times through the large loop. The larger the hole, the more stitches will be required to fill it

Fig 6 *Twisted Corded Buttonhole stitch worked in blocks. This pattern is called Venetian filling.*

Point d'Ireland

Irish needle point lace began at the Presentation Convent in Youghal, County Cork, where Mother Mary Ann Smith had unpicked some Italian lace in order to learn the technique of making it. She began to teach the local women and a lace school was established.

Initially, the lace looked very like the Italian laces but, with the help of an excellent designer, the Irish lace soon developed its own characteristics.

The lace was a flat type, without a raised, outlining edge. Solid areas of the design were opened up with holes to form diamond shapes (a design feature often found in Venetian laces), and the open fillings were in single or double Brussels ground, sometimes decorated with tiny rings. Flowers were either stylised or naturalistic, and leaves always serrated, like rose leaves. Shamrocks were occasionally used in designs.

The Irish lacemakers developed a large number of filling stitches, mostly adapted from other laces of the period.

Point d'Ireland quickly became very popular and was patronised by British royalty during the nineteenth-century lace revival. The lace is still made at Presentation Convent, although in limited quantities. The quality and standard of work, however, remains high.

The handkerchief pictured was made in the late nineteenth century and is one of a set that belonged to Queen Mary's mother, the Duchess of Cambridge. The corner motif has been abstracted for you to work but enlarged to suit modern threads.

Materials required

Architect's or draughtsman's tracing linen (or use coloured paper with self-adhesive film applied to one side)
Fabric for backing
Basting thread
Stranded embroidery cotton
Thread: Choose from Gütermans pure silk 100/3; Madeira No 30; DMC Retours d'Alsace 20 or 30

Preparation for working

Trace the design (Fig 1) and transfer to the tracing linen. Needle-prick the design lines, pricking 2mm (1/16in) apart. Baste the pricked pattern to doubled fabric.

Nineteenth-century Point d'Ireland lace

Working the design

Couch a double thread along the design lines, including leaf veins, inner petals and openings, but omitting the ground bars and the circles for Buttonhole rings.

Work the large flower in Corded Buttonhole stitch with a diamond pattern of holes (see detail, Fig 2). Work the first hole in the position of the dot by missing 2 stitches.

On the 2nd row, work 3 stitches into the hole but make a hole on either side. On the 3rd row, make 3 stitches into the holes, and make holes on either side and above the centre (Fig 3).

Work the half leaves and the alternate petals of the small flowers in Corded Buttonhole stitch but, on the lines of the veins, work a row of holes, missing 1 stitch only. Catch in the trace thread vein as you work.

Work Single Brussels stitch (refer to Fig 3b on page 43), in the large flower openings and in the other petals of the small flowers.

Work stalks, and put in the ground bars. Make Buttonhole Rings for the flowers centres and some very small rings to attach to the fillings where marked on the pattern (Fig 1).

Work Knotted Edge stitch (Fig 4) round the entire design edge, over the trace thread.

Finishing

Release the lace from the fabric by cutting the basting threads and couching thread. The motif is attached to fabric by working a light Buttonhole stitch on the edges.

Detail from the handkerchief showing the abstracted motif

Fig 1 *Trace-off pattern for the motif*

Fig 2 *Diamond pattern of holes on the flower, indicated by an arrangement of dots and, detailed, the stitch formation to work the holes*

Fig 3 *Corded Buttonhole stitch, worked to the arrangement of holes for the diamond pattern*

Fig 4 *Knotted Edge stitch: Work a Buttonhole stitch into the edge, pull up the thread and work 3 more stitches in the loop formed. Pull up gently, make another Buttonhole stitch. Up to 5 stitches can be worked for a bolder edge*

Tape Lace

The use of woven tapes to form patterns dates from the early beginnings of bobbin lace. The technique was given various names – Renaissance lace and Point lace among them. The woven tape was simple to make and it was used to form continuous patterns that were then filled with either needlemade or bobbin stitches. Tape lace was very common in all the lacemaking areas of Italy, Belgium and France in the sixteenth and seventeenth centuries, but its popularity declined in the eighteenth century.

When machine-made tapes became available in the nineteenth century, tape lace revived again as a quicker form of lacemaking. There were many styles and widths of tape available, and some had decorative holes or picot edges.

A thriving industry in Tape lace was set up in the 1860s in Branscombe in South Devon. Bobbin lacemaking was well established and making tape lace was started as a profitable side line for the Devon laceworkers when Honiton lace was in a decline. Tape lace was quicker and easier to make. It is likely that the lace was introduced by John Tucker, a local businessman already in the lace industry. The tape, which was imported from Paris, was of a very fine quality, so the lace produced was similarly of a very high standard and compared favourably with Honiton lace.

John Tucker, using cottage workers, operated his business on what would today be called the 'truck system'. Workers were paid with goods and not with money, and this often caused them great hardship. The system was abolished in 1911.

The Branscombe tape lace differed from others in the variety of filling stitches that were used. This probably occurred because the Honiton workers were accustomed to making elaborate fillings and they employed the same techniques in tape lace. Most of the fillings had been copied from old needle lace designs anyway, and more were invented by the skilful Honiton lacemakers.

Branscombe tape lace was soon in greater demand than Honiton lace.

During the Edwardian period in England, at the beginning of the twentieth century, bold tape lace was very popular for dress trim. The skirt pictured was probably made haute couture. It is made of cream-coloured silk, with silk padded embroidery, and with tape lace worked on a custom-made cream silk tape. The stitches used, however, are very simple. The tape is held in patterns with a loose figure-of-eight stitchery (Fig 1). The motif, abstracted from the skirt lace, would be ideal for inserting into a sleeve or a neckline, or as godets in a soft-fabric skirt.

Materials required
Architect's or draughtsman's tracing linen
Basting cotton
1.50m (1⅝yd) of lace tape for each motif
Thread: Choose from Coton Perlé 12; Coton à Broder; DMC fil a Dentelle; stranded embroidery cotton (match thread to tape colour)

Preparation for working
The working side of the work is the wrong side, so that joins in the tape do not show from the right side.

Trace the motif from Fig 1 onto tracing linen.

Edwardian silk skirt with tape lace decoration

Working the design

Beginning at A, baste the tape to the pattern with short stitches. The tape should lie absolutely flat, turning back on itself to change direction. Finish the first tape at B and start a new tape at C–D.

The stitch used to join the tapes is a loosely worked Faggoting stitch. The needle does not go into the pattern – the stitches lie on the surface.

Make 9 Couronnes (Buttonhole Rings, (page 45, Fig 2), and attach these to each other and to the tapes.

Work Buttonhole-stitched Bars, with Bullion Picot Knots (page 33, Fig 5), in the positions marked.

Remove the basting threads and the piece is ready for insertion.

Detail of the skirt showing the abstracted motif

Fig 1 *Trace the motif onto tracing linen*

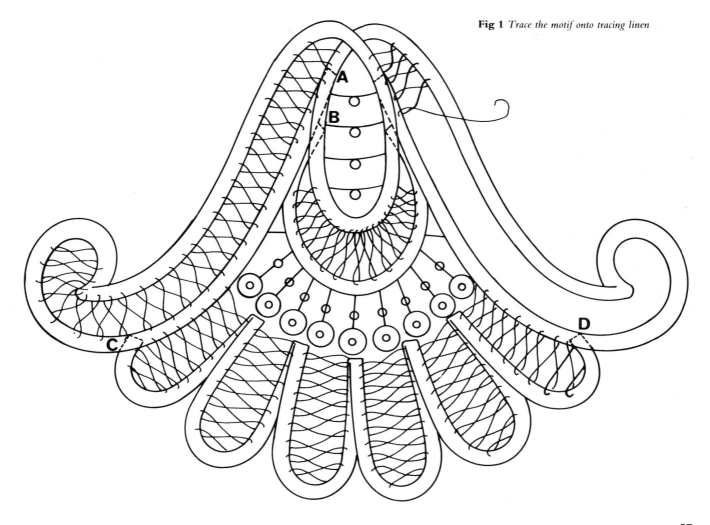

57

Branscombe Point

The collar pictured is of the Branscombe type of lace but was probably made by a home needlewoman, working from the many printed patterns that were available in the mid-nineteenth century. It has many of the features of Branscombe lace, numerous fillings and spider formations, but it has a thicker thread applied to the tape afterwards and also has an added machine-made picot edge and these would not be present in true Branscombe tape lace.

The needle stitches used in Branscombe tape lace were given names that described the design, or sometimes the name of the worker who made it – Zigzag, Holey, Double net, Charlotte's, Eliza's or Little Jessie's.

The motif abstracted from the collar pictured could be used to decorate all kinds of table linens, or could be inserted, or applied, to linen towels. It would look charming inserted into a delicate blouse or, even, a finely-worked wool sweater.

If the motif is being applied or inserted, use the three-sided Triangular Lace stitch, page 95, Figs 1–5. The stitch can be used on straight or curved edges.

Materials required
Architect's or draughtsman's tracing linen
Basting thread
1.80m (2yd) of size 6 lace tape, narrow width, for each motif
Thread: Choose from stranded embroidery cotton (use 1 thread); Madeira No 30; DMC Retours d'Alsace 20 or 30

Collars like this were often made from the printed patterns which were available to needlewomen in the mid-nineteenth century

Fig 1 *Trace-off pattern for the Branscombe Point motif*

Preparation for working

Trace the motif from Fig 1 onto tracing linen.

Working the design

Baste the braid along the design lines, using a diagonal basting stitch which prevents narrower tapes from pulling. The flower is made of one piece of tape, and a second piece is joined for the leaf. Turn the tape on itself at corners and keep the tape smooth on curves.

Whip the edges of the tape on the inside edges of curved lines and pull the thread up slightly to gather the stitches.

Work Double Brussels filling stitch (page 43, Fig 3a) in the open spaces, taking the thread under and over the loops in the tape. The direction is indicated in one of the petals (Fig 1).

Work Spider fillings (Fig 2) in the marked positions. Lay the diagonal threads first, and then whip them back. On the last diagonal, whip to the place where the threads cross, and weave round.

Work Whipped bars in the curved stalk where indicated (Fig 3).

Work Buttonhole-stitched bars with picots where indicated.

Work the flower centre in a filling stitch of your choice.

Work the outside edge in Knotted Edge stitch (page 55, Fig 4).

Finishing

Remove the basting threads and release the lace.

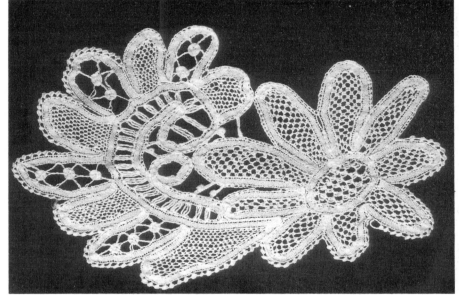

Detail from the collar, showing the stylised flower motif

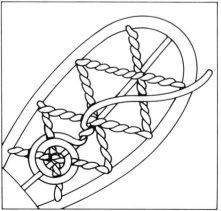

Fig 2 *Spider filling, worked in the petals*

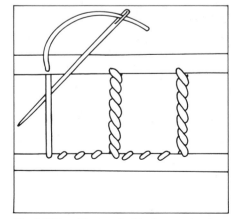

Fig 3 *Whipped bar, worked in the curved stalk*

BRANSCOMBE POINT COLLAR

This pretty collar is typical of Brans-combe Point tape lace, with Whipped bars and Spider fillings. Two attractive fillings are given for you to try for the collar but any of the filling stitches on previous pages could be used.

Materials required
Architect's or draughtsman's tracing linen (or use paper with self-adhesive film on one side)
Basting thread
3m (3¼yd) lace tape
Thread: Choose from Madeira No 30; DMC Retours d'Alsace No 30; stranded embroidery cotton (1 thread used)

The collar fastens at the back of the neck with a tape loop and button

Refer to this picture while working the pattern opposite

Preparation for working
Trace the collar pattern (Fig 1) onto tracing linen. Baste the tape along the design lines, following the techniques described on pages 56–59.

Working the design
Work Whipped bars and Spider fillings where indicated on the pattern. Either of the Pyramid fillings given here can be used, or choose one of the fillings from previous pages.

Pyramid filling A
1st row: Work an even row of Button-hole stitches.
2nd row: Work 2 Buttonhole stitches, miss 2 loops of previous row.
3rd row: Work 1 Buttonhole stitch into the 2 stitches of the previous row.
4th row: Repeat 1st row, working 3 stitches into each large loop (Fig 2).

Pyramid filling B
1st row: Work an even row of Button-hole stitches.
2nd row: Work 4 Buttonhole stitches, miss 2 loops, all the way across.
3rd row: Work 3 Buttonhole stitches into the loops between the 4 stitches of the previous row.
4th row: Work 2 Buttonhole stitches

Fig 1 *Trace-off pattern for the Branscombe Point tape lace collar. Match the two sections on the design lines*

into the loops of the 3 stitches of the previous row.

5th row: Work 1 stitch into the loops of the 2 stitches of the previous row, and 5 stitches into the large loop. Repeat from 2nd row, but alternate the Pyramids (Fig 3). These fillings are very suitable for large spaces in designs.

Finishing

Release the collar from the pattern. Sew a small button to the back neck to correspond with the tape loop.

Fig 2 *Pyramid filling A*

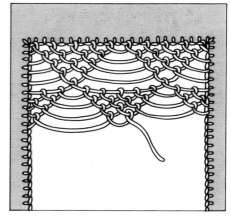

Fig 3 *Pyramid filling B*

CHAPTER FOUR

BOBBIN LACE – THE OTHER ART FORM

It is difficult to refer to the art of lacemaking without mentioning bobbin lace. The techniques of making it are entirely different to all forms of needle lace, but in the history of lace, bobbin lace was as important a part of the textile industry over the centuries.

The origins of bobbin lace lie in weaving. Both spinning and weaving were carried out in the homes of small communities and bobbin lace developed as a form of off-loom weaving. Instead of the warp threads being fastened to a loom, they hang free with a weighted bobbin holding each thread, keeping the thread taut.

A pair of threads, called 'weavers', are woven through the warp threads, called 'passives', just as they would on a loom, but because the warp threads are free to move, open patterns can be formed by twisting or plaiting them.

Bobbin lace is worked from a prepared pattern called a 'pricking', which is attached with pins to a rock-hard, firmly-stuffed pillow or cushion. The pricked-out design shows the crossing of threads, the pinholes being close together where a net pattern is being made and wide spaces edged with holes indicating the solidly woven areas.

The thread is wound onto bobbins, small, shaped pieces of wood, with a slip knot to hold the thread to the bobbin securely, but allowing it to slowly unwind under the bobbin's weight. Bobbin threads hang in pairs from a line of pins at the start of a pattern. As each crossing is made, a pin is placed in the pre-pricked holes to support the threads, and so a lace fabric is built up.

From Belgium to Italy and France

Bobbin lace may have started in Flanders as this was the centre of the European weaving trade and linen thread was produced there. It developed alongside the needle lace industry but, as the origins were humble, the lace was used on simple woven garments, such as shirts, and on sleeves and coifs.

The first designs produced were plaited rather than woven – geo-

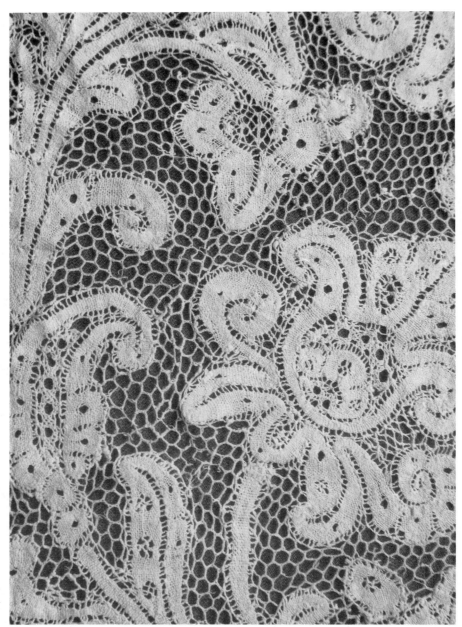

Piece lace with an added background, seventeenth-century Flanders

metric, spiky-looking patterns that endeavoured to copy the needle lace edgings. As techniques developed and fashion changed, finer threads were used, and designs were improved. The techniques for bobbin lace spread from Belgium into France and Italy and the towns and cities where the lace was made became associated with certain types of patterns – Malines, Bruges, Brussels, Valenciennes, Chantilly and Lille. Many variations of patterns could be made by using different combinations of twisting and plaiting and the laces produced in these centres varied from the others in both pattern and style.

Production speeded up

Bobbin lace production developed in two ways – as straight, or one-piece lace, and as motif, or piece lace. Straight lace is the oldest form with many bobbins used, one for each thread, and areas of the design, both the open net work and the solid, woven areas, are worked at the same time.

Motif lace is made as a number of small pieces using only a few bobbins, the pieces hooked or linked together with plaited bars or a net ground.

Both forms of lace production existed in Belgium. Brussels made a piece lace, while Valenciennes, Malines (Mechlin), and Binche made straight laces. Chantilly and Lille also made straight laces.

A waistcoat of Chantilly bobbin lace, mid-nine-teenth century (Rijksmuseum, Amsterdam)

Honiton lace made in the last quarter of the nine-teenth century (Victoria and Albert Museum, London, Crown Copyright)

Once bobbin lace became an industry and demand grew, it became necessary to speed up production. Although one lacemaker could make small pieces using either method, larger items, such as shawls, dress flounces, curtains etc, were a different matter. The same method of production that had been adopted for needle lace making was introduced, with specialists working on one or more stages of production. Speeding up straight lace production was a more difficult problem and was finally solved in Chantilly. It was found that by using an embroidery stitch called Point de Raccroc, a loose, joining stitch, two pieces of lace could be put together with no visible sign of the join. Lace could be made in strips of suitable working width – usually 5cm (2in) – which were then put together by embroiderers to form a whole piece. Even the flowing flower designs with shaded petal effects could be worked by the strip method.

Unfortunately, the joins became visible with age and in fragile, antique pieces of bobbin lace the joins are the first places to show wear.

By the eighteenth century bobbin lace, like needle lace, was at its best both in design and execution. It was soft and draped well, and could be used for dress flounces, aprons, sleeve ruffles and collars. Bobbin lace designers were probably the finest of their time, and must have understood the technique well to have been able to produce patterns that were so beautifully interpreted by the lacemakers.

The English lace industry

The religious persecutions in Europe during the sixteenth and seventeenth centuries led to the exodus of many lacemakers from the continent of Europe and Britain was the nearest, most hospitable country. Lacemakers from Belgium settled in South Devon bringing with them the techniques of piece lace. Those from France went to Buckinghamshire, Bedfordshire and to Northamptonshire in the Midlands, taking the straight lace techniques.

In the Devon countryside, bobbin lace making became a cottage industry, the trade centre being Honiton. Honiton lace, although very like Brussels lace, developed a style of its own and became the most

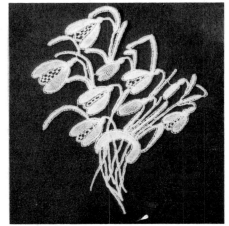

Snowdrops motif in Honiton Lace, early twentieth century (Exeter Museum, Devon)

Left: a pricking for a bobbin lace edging; middle: first stage of working; right: second stage of working

64

Bobbin lace in working on a pillow

famous of the English laces. The flowers and insects of the Devon countryside were used as design inspiration and, with newly-invented stitch combinations and very fine thread, Honiton lace became as sought-after as any produced in Europe.

Individual motifs were supplied to home workers weekly by the lace trader who collected the finished motifs the following week. It was said that a lacemaker could earn as many shillings as covered her piece of lace. The motifs then went to another group of workers for assembly into collars, cuffs, ruffles, veils etc.

Honiton enjoyed royal patronage and was commissioned to produce the lace for Queen Victoria's wedding dress in 1840. A group of 200 lacemakers at Beer worked from March until November and the cost of the lace was £1000. This achievement improved Honiton's trade and the lace reached its peak of excellence and value at the Great Exhibition in London in 1851 when a finely worked piece, exhibited by J. Tucker & Co of Branscombe, fetched £3000. Honiton lace unfortunately went into a decline

towards the end of the century, mainly due to a lack of good designers. Design improved around 1897 and there was a revival in the industry. Links with the Royal Family were maintained, with Devon lacemakers presenting lace wedding gifts for the royal weddings, a traditional that still exists today.

The straight laces that were developed in the Midlands bore a very strong resemblance to the laces of Lille and Chantilly, and many of the stitch combinations were the same. At the peak of production in the nineteenth century, the 'piece-work' strip method was adopted for large shawls and veils.

In the Northamptonshire region, the style of the lace changed when the early machine-made laces began to appear. The ground was no longer net but consisted of plaited bars and leaf shapes. This proved a popular form and the same style of lace was developed in Malta and in Le Puy in France.

The romance of bobbins

Bobbins are the essential item in lacemakers' equipment and vary in

style from country to country. Continental bobbins have bulbous ends to provide additional weight but those used by the English Honiton workers were fine and pointed. The technique the workers used required that bobbins pass through loops in the lace when joining pieces and the thread was so light that little weight was required. Buckinghamshire bobbins, on the other hand, were short and fat, known as 'Bucks Thumps' but these were gradually replaced by those usually thought of as 'English' bobbins – slender, with weight added with beads, called 'spangles'.

Bobbins, to a lacemaker, often represented the story of her life. Each phase or happening, good or bad, could be seen on her pillow. Love messages, religious tracts, dates of weddings and births, and deaths, were inscribed on the bobbins.

It was said that, when a lacemaker's husband died, her entire pillow went into mourning, with black beads on the bobbins.

CHAPTER FIVE

EMBROIDERED LACE

The technique of making fine, knotted net using a needle or shuttle developed from the ancient net-making techniques of fishermen. Patterns were darned on the basic silk- or linen-thread net and Lacis, as it was called, was used for dress decoration, for home furnishings, and by the church.

Lacis was frequently decorated with metal threads and coloured silks, and was sometimes used in conjunction with simple cutwork and Reticella designs. The importance of Lacis is reflected in the number of sixteenth-century pattern books which featured the lace, and the same patterns were reprinted again and again for three hundred years.

A new industry begins

The first knitting machine, invented by the Reverend William Lee in 1598 and intended by him for the production of machine-made silk stockings, was not really developed until 1758 when there was a commercial need for a net that resembled the bobbin and needle lace grounds. With constant research, a successful machine evolved and, by 1810, there were 18,000 frames in Nottingham producing a net with an hexagonal mesh. A whole new industry had begun, with 1500 women and children spotting or needle-running nets in Nottingham alone.

The net was a very stretchy fabric, made of silk threads, but the invention of the warp frame meant that cotton could also be used. This machine combined conventional weaving with the knitting machine technique and, instead of a single thread, the machine now had warp threads, as on a loom. This was an important breakthrough. John Heathcoat's bobbin net machine could produce net in wider widths than before and was nearer in appearance and feel to the hand-made nets. The piece lace industries began to use it to attach motifs and the terms 'Honiton Applied' and 'Brussels Applied' were used to describe the laces. The scale of production enabled applied and needle-run laces to be produced comparatively cheaply, and embroidered lace was produced in all the lacemaking centres of Europe. The boom came at a time when simple styles and diaphanous fabrics were in fashion.

The net-making machine was to be followed by machines that could make good reproductions of almost any type of lace, particularly the bobbin varieties such as Chantilly. For the hand-made lace industries, the end was in sight.

Lacemaking at the Convent of Poor Clares, Kenmare, Ireland. Nuns were diligent in maintaining the quality of Irish lace and it is due to them that the industry has continued into the twentieth century

Limerick Lace

The embroidered net industry in Ireland was set up by an Englishman, Charles Walker. Having married the daughter of a net manufacturer, Charles Walker moved to Limerick from Essex, England, taking twenty-four lace embroiderers with him. Mr and Mrs Walker taught the skills to the local Irish, who took enthusiastically to the skills of needle-running and tambour work and by 1842, when the potato famine devastated Ireland, the industry was well established.

Limerick lace gradually spread to other parts of Ireland and the work force employed in its production ran into thousands. Pieces were shown at the Great Exhibition in London in 1851, and were awarded medals which further boosted demand for the lace.

Design was improved in the late nineteenth century and there was some experimentation in copying designs from the old Brussel's bobbin and needle laces. New, original designs for Limerick lace also evolved, often featuring the Shamrock, Rose or Harp but, as needle-run lace was being produced in most European lace centres and designs were copied everywhere, it is often difficult to identify an old piece of lace as being made in Ireland.

The beauty of Limerick lace is its delicacy, and the contrast between the outlines of the design and the fillings stitches used within small areas – called 'caskets'.

A great many different stitches can be used in this lace but it is sometimes better to restrict a design to just a few. Workers in the Irish lace industry always made a sampler so that decisions could be made about the best stitch or stitches for a particular design.

The veil pictured is nineteenth century and a motif has been abstracted for you to work. It would look superb used as border for a Christening robe or could be used as an insert on a tablecloth. A trace-off pattern for the motif is on page 74. The motif worked in an embroidery ring is pictured opposite.

Materials required
Architect's tracing linen
Cotton net
Thread: Coarse thread such as Coton à Broder or Sylko Perlé 12; fine thread such as stranded embroidery cotton, or Madeira No 30 or 50
Ball-pointed or crewel needle
A large embroidery frame or ring

Preparing for working
Trace the design from Fig 1, page 74 onto the tracing linen and ink over the lines so that they can be clearly seen through the net. The embroidery frame should be large enough to take the entire design. If a square frame is being used, prepare the edges of the net with fabric strips and lace them to the side struts. If a sufficiently large embroidery ring is being used, bind the rings with cotton binding.

Stretch the net on the frame or in the embroidery ring.

Place the design under the net and baste the two together, working the basting lines round the edges and between the design lines.

Working the design
The outlining is worked first. Thread the needle with as long a length of thread as you can possibly manage. Work can begin at any point. Lift a bar of net and work a stitch over it twice. Go along the design lines, taking the needle under and over alternate net bars, and keeping the thread fairly loose. It may sometimes be necessary to miss a bar to keep the line smooth and prevent angles forming. The beauty of Limerick depends on the care taken at this stage.

Nineteenth-century Limerick lace wedding veil

To fasten off the thread, take a stitch to form a loop, pass the needle through the loop and pull up to form a knot, then repeat the action.

When starting new threads, whip the new over the old for about 18mm (³⁄₄in) and then continue working.

Complete the outlining of the design and then unpick the basting threads to remove the pattern.

Needlerun fillings
Fillings fall into two groups, all-over patterning and linear. Two all-over patterns and two linear are illustrated in the stitch diagrams below.

Darning
The areas which are closely filled are the main design shapes and can be worked in several ways to achieve the denseness required. Darning is worked to include the outline stitches but should not be taken beyond them. (See E and F in the diagrams below.) Treble darning, which is not illustrated, combines Single darning and Double darning and produces a dense effect.

Edging
The simplest finish is worked by darning in a coarse thread, either to the shape of the net edge (zigzagged or straight) or in scallops (see G, below).

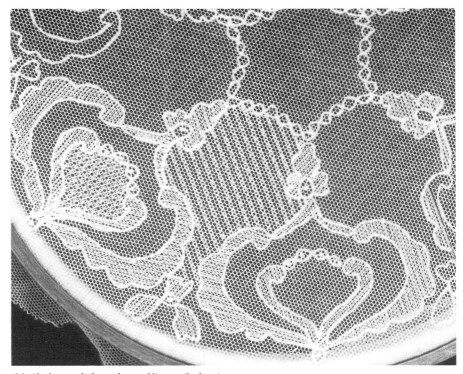

Motif abstracted from the wedding veil showing outline darning, Single darning, Cobweb filling and Cross stitch filling

Horizontal Whip stitch *Working left to right, whip the thread over the net holes.* (A)
Cross stitch *Whip over the net holes from left to right in the first stage, then over the same holes from right to left in the second stage.* (B)
Wave stitch *Darn the thread under vertical bars of the net over three rows of holes.* (C)
Cobweb stitch *Darn the thread behind two bars, alternating over three rows of holes for the first row,* then work the second row in the same way, reversed, into the centre. (D)
Edge finish *Darn a coarse trace thread into a scalloped pattern, work Buttonhole stitches over the thread.*
Diagonal Darning (Single darning) *Darn the thread through the net holes once.* (E)
Straight darning (Double darning) *Darn the thread through the same net holes twice.* (F).

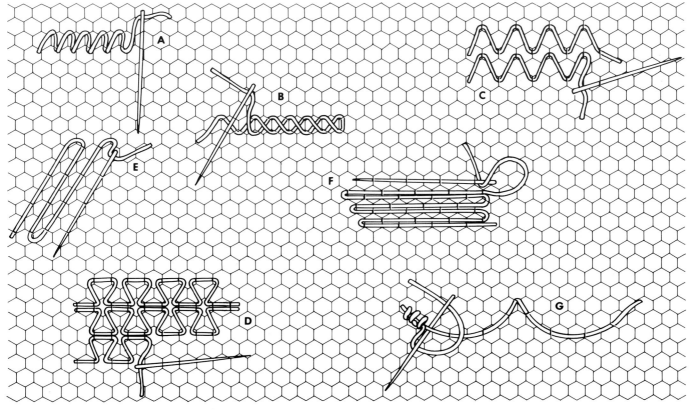

Carrickmacross Lace

The working technique of Carrickmacross lace involves the application of muslin to fine net, and then parts are cut away to reveal a design with open areas that are filled with needle-run stitches.

The introduction of this technique into Ireland has been attributed to Mrs Grey Porter who saw work of this type in Italy while on her honeymoon. Mrs Porter taught it to her maid, applying muslin to the newly-invented machine-made net – and a new type of lace was created.

The lace was not fully developed until the potato famine when industry for the distressed Irish was of paramount importance. The managers of the Bath and Shirley estates in Carrickmacross village turned an empty house into a lace school and, before long, there were more schools providing tuition for local women.

There was a need for a high standard of work, and this required supervision. Various lace centres were set up to control both the teachers and the workers. Towards the end of the century, the work was being taught by the nuns from St Louis Convent, who made sure that the quality of the lace was maintained.

The lace does not launder well and was not, therefore, as popular as Limerick lace but it was in demand for accessories such as fans and parasols, and for collars.

The parasol pictured is an example of mixed techniques; some parts are cut as guipure with needle bars while other areas are applied to net. The pattern from the lower edge has been abstracted for a collar.

The traditional fabrics for Carrickmacross were a fine, semi-transparent muslin or cambric, and a square- or diamond-mesh net. These are not now easily obtainable, so substitutions must be made.

Natural fibres must be used together and not mixed with man-made fibres. Cotton organdie should be used with cotton net or silk tulle, and

Lace parasol from which the Carrickmacross motif has been abstracted

nylon organza with nylon net.

The net most easily available is hexagonal and the fillings recommended for the collar are shown worked on this.

Materials required
50cm (20in) square of organdie
50cm (20in) square of cotton net
Coarse threads, such as Sylko Perlé 12; Coats Chain-Mercer Crochet cotton No 40; Coton à Broder
Fine thread for filling, such as Brok 110; Honiton thread 120; Madeira No 30 or 50
Stranded embroidery cotton (use 1 thread for couching)
Architect's – tracing linen

Preparation for working
Pre-wash the organdie and net to soften and shrink them. Trace the half-collar pattern from Fig 2 on page 75, re-tracing for the other half and matching the design. Trace the collar onto the tracing linen, leaving at least 25mm (1in) allowance all round. Place the net on top of the design, and then place the organdie on the net. Baste all three layers together on the edges, keeping the layers as smooth as possible. Baste between the design lines also, to keep the layers together, but do not work basting stitches over the design lines.

The design is couched with a double coarse thread and there should be no joins in the thread. You will need about 4m (4¾yd). Double the length of thread and attach the loop end at A (Fig 2, page 75) with a few stitches using the fine thread. Make the stitches through the net and organdie only, not the pattern.

Lay one coarse (trace) thread along the design line and couch over it,

through the organdie and the net, using fine thread, making small, close, oversewing stitches. Work down one side of the figure-of-eight border to B, making picots on the outer edge (Fig 1 this page).

Bring the other end of the trace thread down the other side of the design line to B, and then take one thread of the trace thread each side of the flower, crossing threads and stitching the point firmly.

Work the petal separating lines by doubling the thread back on itself and oversewing the two together (Fig 2 this page). Take the thread in a figure-of-eight on the inside of the flower and at C, cross the threads, sewing firmly, taking one thread to the left and one to the right to complete the leaf, with threads coming together again at D. Continue working the doubled trace thread in this way, working all the design lines.

If, due to miscalculation, it becomes necessary to join in a new trace thread, overlap the ends of old and new for about 12mm (½in) and continue with oversewing.

Couching threads are fastened off by working oversewing back for about 12mm (½in).

Remove the basting stitches from the lace and lift the fabric from the paper pattern.

Working the design
This is a most important stage and the work must be done slowly and carefully. One careless snip, and the piece is ruined.

Using the finger tips, lift the organdie sections that are to be cut away from the net and snip into it with the scissors points. Cut away the organdie close to the couched design lines but taking care not to cut the

Detail from the parasol edge

net. Cut away the areas of net in the same way (refer to the detail photograph). Do not cut fabric away from the area surrounding the collar design.

Work Limerick filling stitches in the centres of the flowers and leaves (refer to the diagrams on pages 68–69). Work Buttonhole-stitched bars on the petals of the larger flower. Cut away the net and organdie under the bars. Work Twirls (Fig 3) on the net where indicated.

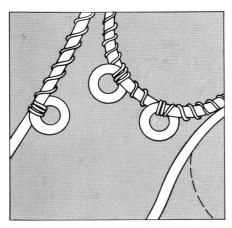

Fig 1 *Picots worked with trace thread and couching*

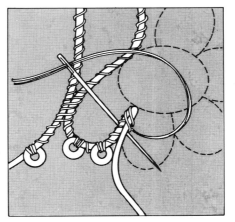

Fig 2 *Double the trace thread on itself on the petals*

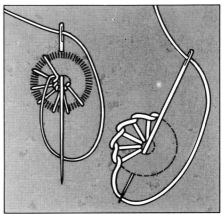

Fig 3 *Two kinds of Twirl: work with the knot on the inside of the circle, or on the outside edge*

CARRICKMACROSS HANDKERCHIEF

Handkerchiefs with lace edges were a popular fashion accessory during the eighteenth century and were flourished, and used flirtatiously, rather in the same way as a fan. Gentlemen tended to leave a handkerchief trailing from a coat pocket, or from a cuff, showing off yet another piece of exquisite lace. Handkerchiefs became smaller in size in the nineteenth century and lace-trimmed handkerchiefs were often made for wedding accessories. The handkerchief pictured is early twentieth century. One corner only is shown, but all four corners are worked with Carrickmacross lace. The decorative part is an integral part of the handkerchief and does not therefore require to be attached.

Materials required
45cm (18in) square of organdie
45cm (18in) square of cotton net
Coarse threads, such as Sylko Perlé 12; Coats Chain-Mercer Crochet cotton No 40; Coton à Broder
Fine thread for filling, such as Brok 110; Honiton thread 120; Madeira No 30 or 50
Stranded embroidery cotton (use 1 strand for couching)
Architect's or draughtsman's tracing linen
Scissors: if possible, these should be Carrickmacross scissors, which have one pointed blade and one rounded blade (see Suppliers, page 96). Alternatively, use sharp-pointed embroidery scissors

Preparation for working
Trace the pattern (Fig 1) four times to make a square pattern. Trace the pattern on the tracing linen, allowing at least 25mm (1in) round the design. Couch the coarse thread round all the design lines, following the procedure described for the collar (pages 70–71). Lift the fabric from the pattern.

Work filling stitches, referring to the diagrams on page 69. Work the holes in the central scroll using the technique described on page 19, Fig 2 for broderie Anglaise.

Finishing
Cut away the net behind the handkerchief centre, and cut away the organdie from the inside areas of the bow.

Work Buttonhole Rings (page 45, Fig 2) where indicated on the pattern.

Other uses for the motif
The corner motif, Fig 2, could also be worked on an organdy tray or table-cloth ribbons and flowers, would make charming wedding gifts.

Fig 1 *Trace-off pattern for the Carrickmacross handkerchief. Trace the design 4 times to make a square pattern*

CARRICKMACROSS MOTIFS

The triangular pattern (Fig 2) is for a small piece of Carrickmacross lace which could be used as an insert for a traycloth or a trolley cloth. It could also look extremely pretty set into the front of a boat-shaped neckline on a summer blouse or dress.

The materials required are as for the collar on pages 70–71.

Preparing for working

Trace the pattern on tracing linen, allowing at least 25mm (1in) round the design. Couch the coarse thread round the design lines following the procedure given for the collar on pages 70–71.

When working the couching begin the doubled trace thread at A (see pattern), and take one end to the left and one to the right to meet and cross at B. Work along both sides to C, cross the threads and outline the flower, making a figure-of-eight centre. Work the figure-of-eight with picots, following Fig 2, page 71 for the technique.

Working the design

Lift the fabrics from the pattern, as described on pages 70–71 for the collar, and cut the organdie and the net areas. Work filling stitches from the diagrams on page 69. Cut the excess fabric away from around the insert.

The original handkerchief from which the corner motif is abstracted

Fig 2 *Triangular pattern for Carrickmacross lace which could be used for an insert on a traycloth or for a dress neckline*

73

This triangular motif has also been abstracted from the veil on pages 68–69. It is an ideal shape for working on handkerchiefs or scarves, or would make a pretty neckline insert

Fig 1 *Trace-off pattern for the Limerick lace motif described on pages 68–69. The motif could be used as a border design for a Christening robe, or could be inserted in exquisite table linens*

Patterns for lacemaking

The trace-off patterns given here, Fig 1 for a Limerick lace motif and Fig 2 for a Carrickmacross lace collar, together with the smaller motifs, are interchangeable on techniques. Each of the patterns can be used for working both laces.

These patterns can also be used for working needle lace, choosing fillings from the many stitches provided in earlier chapters. The patterns could also be adapted to cutwork techniques.

Similarly, the patterns provided in the needle lace chapter can be adapted to embroidered lace techniques.

Once you have studied and understood the methods involved in a specific lacemaking technique, you will begin to appreciate how a design from another source can be utilised. Some embroidery transfers, for instance, pictorial, floral and abstract, can be adapted for lacemaking. All kinds of shapes, linear and flowing, readily adapt themselves to needle lace. The Galleon in lace on pages 48–51 illustrates how shapes of all kinds can be formed in lace.

Traditionally, lace workers made sample books of fillings or needlerun patterns for themselves, keeping them on hand for selection when a new design was being planned.

You might consider making a sample book for yourself, made up of small motifs and using the fillings stitches on previous pages.

Thus, with the many varied patterns for motifs, inserts, collars, handkerchiefs, edgings etc available to you in this book, a rich source of material is yours for practising the art of lacemaking.

Use the small motifs on the opposite page for practise pieces in either Limerick or Carrickmacross lace. Small motifs can be displayed on pincushions (see page 93)

Fig 2 *Trace-off pattern for the Carrickmacross collar*

B

C

A

D

75

Lacis, Netting or Filet

Lacis, or Filet, is probably the earliest form of lace, having developed from the technique used for making fisherman's nets. It has various names, but they all apply to a square or diamond-shaped mesh which is usually re-embroidered.

Lacis was well-established in mediaeval times as a decorative textile and was made in both silk and linen threads to make decorative accessories such as hair nets, girdles, purses and so on, as well as for ecclesiastic garments and furnishings. Surviving pieces are mostly large-sized coverlets or wall hangings, often with Lacis combined with cutwork, such as the curtain pictured.

The popularity of the lace lasted through the centuries until the late nineteenth century when there was an increase in interest. The interest has continued into the twentieth century and the lace is now referred to as 'netting' or 'Filet'. Filet is easily duplicated by machine and with hand-crochet stitches. The latter is referred to as Filet crochet to distinguish the lace from the needlemade variety.

The curtain pictured is late nineteenth or early twentieth century and is made in linen thread, with alternating squares of cutwork. The net and the darning are worked in the same linen thread.

Filet darning is worked on a square knotted net, which is made with a netting shuttle. It can, however, be made with a needle in the same way as other needle laces, and this is particularly useful when making small items or when using a fine thread. The size of the mesh can be adjusted by using different gauges of graph paper, to suit the thread.

A small motif and edging patterns on pages 78–79 are taken from the curtain as practise pieces.

Materials required

Architect's or draughtsman's tracing linen (or use coloured paper with self-adhesive film applied to one side)

Thread: Either DMC 20 or Coats Chain-Mercer Crochet cotton No 60.

Squared graph paper with a grid of 8 squares to 25mm (1in)

Fabric for backing

Preparing for working

Draw an area 11 squares by 11 squares on the tracing linen. Using the graph paper as a guide, mark in the intersecting mesh points. Baste the pattern to doubled fabric. Couch a doubled trace thread round the square, putting in small, slanting basting stitches at the marks on the edge of the square. These support the threads while working the mesh, and ensures that the mesh is of even size.

Left: Nineteenth-century piece of Filet lace and cut-work used for a modern curtain. Above: detail from the curtain showing a Filet section and part of the border pattern

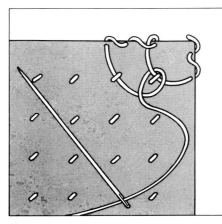

Fig 1 *Filet net: make a Buttonhole stitch through the loop of the previous row*

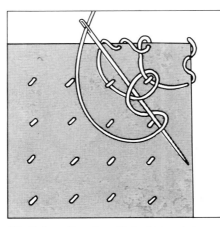

Fig 2 *Stage 2: make a Twisted Buttonhole stitch over the loop*

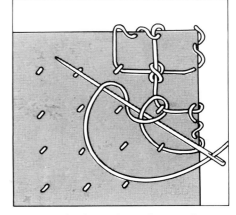

Fig 3 *Work Filet net diagonally across the square from the corner*

Working the design

Attach the working thread to the right hand side and take it through the first slanting basting stitch. Make a Buttonhole stitch over the top bar, and then whip along to the next loop position.

Take the thread through the basted stitch and make a Buttonhole stitch through the loop of the previous row (Fig 1, page 77). Make a Twisted Buttonhole stitch over this loop, as in Fig 2. (Refer to page 25 for Twisted Buttonhole stitch.)

Take the thread through the basted stitch and work a Buttonhole stitch over the bar on the bottom edge. Whip to the next position, through the basting stitch, and continue making Buttonhole stitches and Twisted Buttonhole stitches, on the diagonals (Fig 3 page 77). When the net is completed, remove the basting threads but leave the main, outer square couching threads in position until after darning is completed.

Darning Filet

The darning thread in Filet is continuous and, therefore, careful planning of the route is essential. The starting and finishing points are important to make sure that all parts of the design are worked and a definite sequence is established.

The small motif and edging have the usual features of shape and internal holes so that following the diagrams will enable you to learn the sequence.

The foundation cross is made first and then each segment completed before moving on to the next. The thread is taken in and out of the edge in some places to carry it to the next position and also to strengthen it.

The holes are the important features of the design and they should not have threads passing through them; the edge stitch enables you to avoid this.

Filet is traditionally finished by working Buttonhole stitches on a row of net beyond the design.

Buttonhole-stitch the outer edges of the square and then release the lace from the pattern.

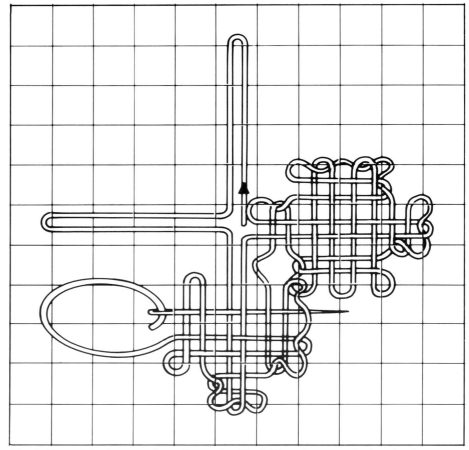

Fig 4 *Above: Filet Darning; the small triangle shows the starting point; follow the direction of threads*

Fig 5 *Top right: Pattern for the Filet edging*

Fig 6 *Bottom right: Pattern for the leaf motif*

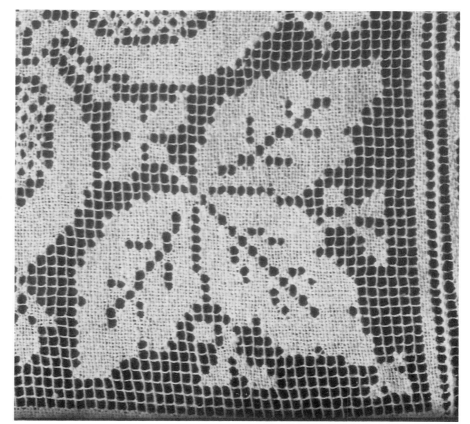

Detail of the leaf motif from the curtain

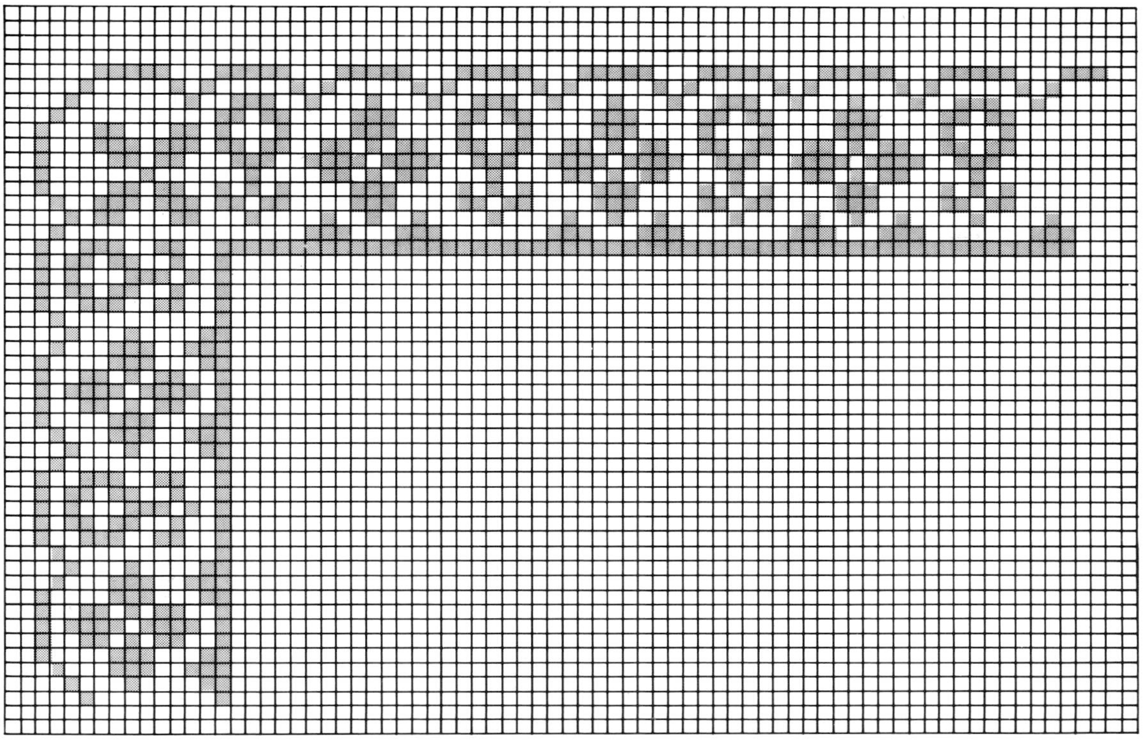

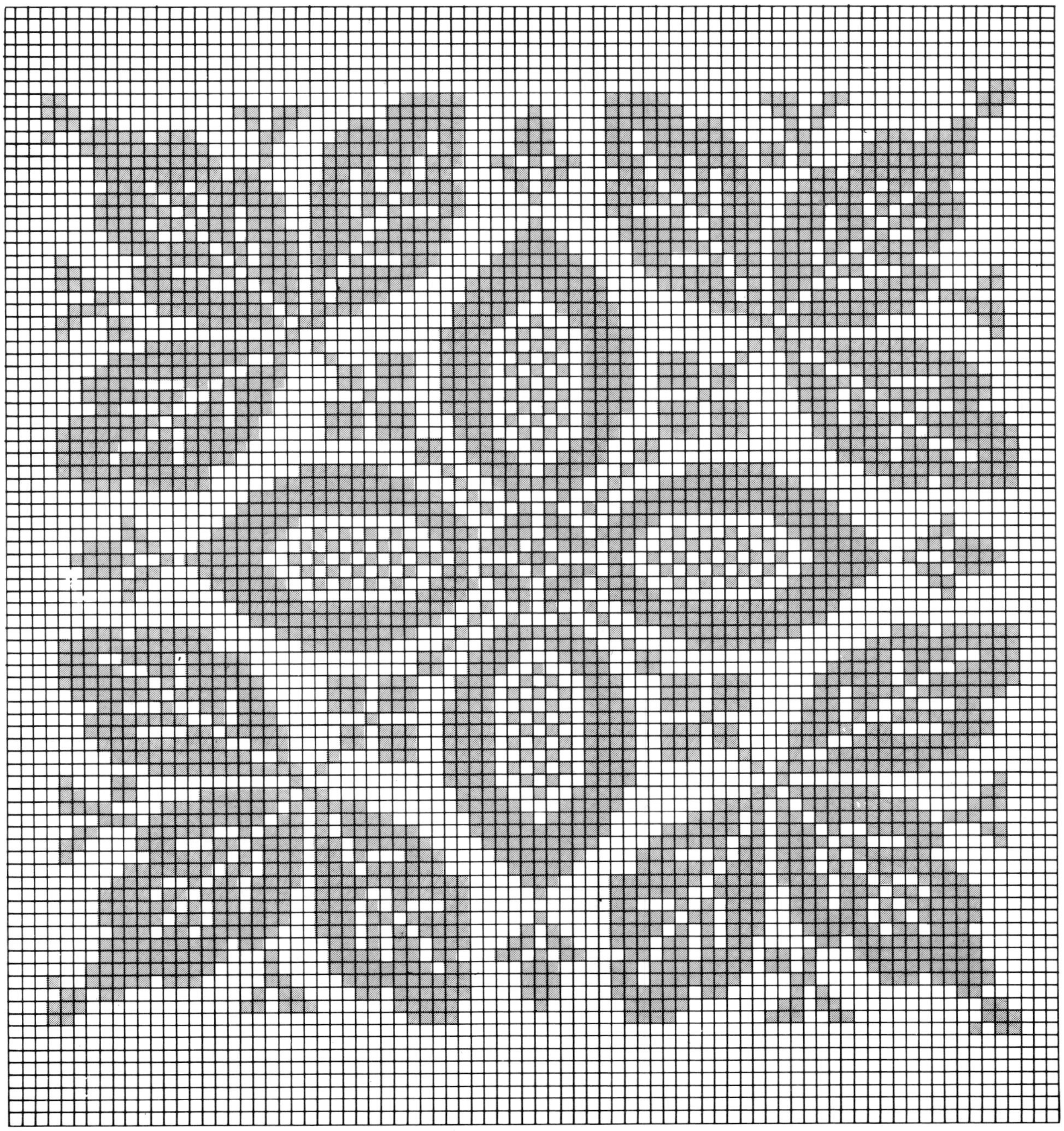

CHAPTER SIX

CROCHETED LACE

The origins of crochet are obscure but the craft seems to have started in France at some time in the seventeenth century. Hooked needles (crochets) were used in the bobbin lace industry to link parts of lace together. It is also possible that crochet developed from tambour work, an embroidery worked with a hook on net, which existed towards the end of the eighteenth century.

Crochet was practised by the French nuns and, the news spreading to their sister nuns in Ireland, Irish girls were sent to France to learn the art. However, the crochet industry did not become established in Ireland until the nineteenth century when the nuns of the Ursuline Convent in Cork began to develop the technique. Soon, crochet was being worked in other parts of Ireland and became a valuable home industry during the time of the Irish Potato Famine.

The Famine was responsible in no small way for the development of Irish crocheted lace. Potatoes were the staple diet of the peasant communities and, during the 1840s, the crop failed with blight for two consecutive years. The peasants could not afford grain for bread, and there was nothing else for them to eat. Many who could afford the cheap passage went to America, where they could earn money to send home to their families, and they went in their thousands. In Ireland, entire villages perished from the fever which followed the famine and the problems multiplied. Volunteers from the English gentry living in Ireland, and others, set up schools with the help of the nuns, to teach the Irish women to crochet lace which was sold in England for famine relief.

There were no written patterns because very few of the Irish could read, and the women worked from pattern samples. Many of these have survived as a record of the women's ingenuity, and it is from these patterns that many of the modern crochet patterns have been derived.

Many of the early designs were copied from the Venetian Gros Point and Rose Point laces and, using crochet stitches, solid areas, open fillings and picot bars, could all be imitated. Irish lace gradually grew in popularity and the motifs recognised today, the Rose, the Wheel, the Shamrock, and stylised flowers, were joined with a crocheted mesh and made into jackets, dresses, collars and household furnishings.

Crochet appealed to Irish women; for the most part they worked in their own cottages, and were free to develop new patterns and stitches. However, this freedom was also a disadvantage in that no overall checks were being made on the standard of their work. Lace was bought by travelling agents and, although a market existed, it was to be short-lived. The poor standard of work was partly to blame, but lacemaking machinery had been invented with the facility of producing heavy needle lace, which crochet resembled.

The industry revived again in the 1890s when heavy lace was again in fashion and efforts were made to improve production standards. Irish crochet was to reach its peak in 1905, when pattern books were available in different languages, and not all the Irish crocheted lace which survives from that time was made in Ireland.

The techniques of Irish crocheted lace travelled with the emigrants to the United States of America and, taken up by American women, became an important and popular pastime. The making of lace edgings for clothes and furnishings in particular was pursued and new stitches and patterns were developed. Some of these were named after traditional patchwork patterns, which in some ways they resembled, Pineapple stitch and Popcorn stitch for example. Over the next 150 years, American women were to develop the craft and American crocheted lace now has its own place in the history of lacemaking.

Men, too, learned to make crocheted lace and this drawing from an American magazine identifies the man as an invalid making lace to support his family

Broughton

HANDKERCHIEF EDGINGS

Crocheted lace is ideal for edging handkerchiefs, or for any item of clothing, or household linen, that is likely to require frequent laundering. The Pointed edging is worked directly onto the fabric edge. Loops and Fan edging and Shell edging are worked to length and then sewn to the fabric.

Materials required
For edging 1 ladies' handkerchief:
1 20g ball of Coats Chain-Mercer Crochet cotton No 60
Crochet hook size .75mm (No 4½)

Abbreviations

ch – chain; dc – double crochet; tr – treble; dbl tr – double treble; lp(s) – loop(s); ss – slip stitch; sp – space; st – stitch. Directions in brackets are worked the number of times stated after the last bracket.

Pointed edging

1st row: Ss into the handkerchief edge at a corner, 8 ch to stand as 1 dbl tr and 4ch, 1 dbl tr into the same hole below, ★ miss about 6mm (¼in) of the edge: rep from ★ to end, making sure there is always a complete V-point at the corners. Ss into the 5th ch.

2nd row: ★ Into next 4 ch lps, work (1

Fine, crocheted lace edgings on delicate handkerchiefs make charming gifts

82

ch, 1 tr) 5 times, 1 ch, 1 dc into next lp; rep from ★ to end. Ss into end.
3rd row: Work 1 dc into every st along the row but when the centre of a scallop is reached, work a lp of 4 ch, then continue in dc to the centre of the next scallop. Fasten off thread.

Loops and Fan edging
Begin by making 12 ch.
1st row: 1 dc into 8th ch from hook, 5 ch, miss 3 ch, 1 tr, 3 ch and 1 tr all into the next ch, 3 ch, turn.
2nd row: 9 tr into 3 ch, sp, 1 dc into next lp, 5 ch, 1 dc into next lp, 7 ch, turn.
3rd row: 1 dc into next lp, 5 ch, miss 4 tr, 1 tr, 3 ch and 1 tr all into next tr, 3 ch, turn.
3rd row: 1 dc into next lp, 5 ch, miss 4 tr, 1 tr, 3 ch and 1 tr all into next tr, 3 ch, turn.
Rep the 2nd and 3rd rows for the length required to go along one edge, ending with a 3rd pattern row.

Corner
1st row: 9 tr into 3 ch, sp, 1 dc into the next lp, 3 ch, 1 dc into the next lp, 5 ch, turn.
2nd row: Miss 4 tr, 1 tr, 3 ch and 1 tr all into next tr, 3 ch, turn.
3rd row: 9 tr into 3 ch, sp, 1 dc into next lp, 3 ch, 1 dc into same corner lp as dc of 1st row, 5 ch, turn.
Rep 2nd and 3rd corner rows once

more, turning with 7 ch on last of these rows.
7th row: 1 dc into 3 ch sp, 5 ch miss 4 tr, 1 tr, 3 ch and 1 tr all into the next tr, 3 ch, turn. Repeat 2nd and 3rd rows of edging until next corner is reached, then turn as before.
Work rem 2 sides in the same way ending with a 2nd pattern row, and omitting turning ch at the end of the last row. Fasten off. Sew ends together.

The outer edging
1st row: Ss into turning ch, lp at tip of 9 tr group, ★ 7 ch, 1 dc into 3 ch at end of next 9 tr group; rep from ★ all round, ending with a ss into first dc.
2nd row: Work 9 dc into each lp, ss into first dc. Fasten off.

Finishing
Sew edging to handkerchief, allowing 2 lps to each corner.

Shell edging
Begin by making 9 ch.
1st row: Make a shell thus; 2 tr into 9th ch from hook, 2 ch, 2 tr into same ch, 5 ch, turn.
2nd row: 2 tr, 2 ch and 2 tr all into 2 ch sp of shell, 5 ch, turn.
Repeat the 2nd row for length required to go round a handkerchief, allowing 2 lps for each corner and making sure that there are an equal

number of lps between, on each side of the handkerchief, and work the last pattern by making 2 tr in 2 ch sp, 1 ch, then join to the beginning thus: remove the hook and insert into 1st ch made and pull the lp through, then 1 ch, 2 tr into same place as last tr, 5 ch, turn and ss into same place as join. Fasten off thread.

The heading
1st row: Ss into a corner lp, 6 ch, (1 dbl tr into the same lp, 2 ch) 5 times, 1 dbl tr into the same lp, ★ (1 dbl tr, 2 ch), 3 times all into the next lp, 1 dbl tr into the same lp, rep from ★ all round; but in the corner work (1 dbl tr, 2 ch) 6 times into the corner lp, 1 dbl tr into the same lp. Ss into 4th of 6 ch at beginning to join.
2nd row: 1 dc into first 2 ch sp of 1st corner (3 ch, 1 dc into next sp) 5 times, ★ 1 dc into next sp, (3 ch, 1 dc) twice into next sp, 3 ch, 1 dc into next sp; rep from ★ all round, but work each corner as given for 1st corner. Ss into 1st dc at beginning to join. Fasten off thread.

Finishing
Sew edging to handkerchief, allowing 2 loops to each corner.

83

THE FLOWER DRESS

This beautiful dress with Irish crocheted lace bodice is perfect for a young girl. The bodice is unmounted and a body stocking should be worn under the dress. Indian cotton was used to make the skirt in the dress pictured, but any soft fabric would do as well – muslin, tulle, lawn, or even silk. The dress was originally made in white, but crochet cotton is available in a range of colours and any may be used.

The bodice has in it all the techniques for Irish crocheted lace. Leaves, flowers and stems are worked in different sizes and the net background is in the traditional, simple form. The bodice is edged with a crocheted scallop bar with picots, which was, originally, a pattern adapted from Venetian laces.

Materials required
5 (6, 6, 6) 20g balls of Coats Chain-Mercer Crochet cotton No 40
Crocket hook 1.00 (No 4)
2.20m (2⅜yd) lightweight fabric 114cm (45in) wide
Seam binding to match the fabric
35cm (14in) zip fastener
Matching sewing thread

Tension
11 loops – 7.5cm (3in), 8 rows – 25mm (1in).

Measurements
To fit bust sizes – 81 (86, 91, 96)cm 32 (34, 36, 38)in.

Abbreviations
ch – chain; dc – double crochet; hlf tr – half treble; tr – treble; dbl tr – double treble; trip tr – triple treble; lp(s) – loop(s); st – stitch) ss – slip stitch; p – picot; rep – repeat; sp – space; patt – pattern.

Back
Commence with 6 ch.
1st Row (right side): 1 dbl tr into 6th ch from hook, (5 ch, 1 dbl tr into top of last dbl tr) 45 (49, 53, 57) times, 5ch, turn.
2nd Row: 1 dc into first lp, ★ 5 ch, 1 dc into next lp; rep from ★ ending with 2 ch, 1 tr into same place as first dbl tr, 1 ch, turn.
3rd Row: 1 dc into first tr, ★ 5 ch, 1 dc into next 5 ch lp; rep from ★ to within turning ch, 5 ch, 1 dc into 3rd of 5 ch, 5 ch, turn.
4th Row: 1 dc into first lp, ★ 5 ch, 1 dc

into next lp; rep from ★ ending with 2 ch, 1 tr into next dc, 1 ch, turn.

3rd Size Only
Next Row: With right side facing attach thread to last dc made on last row before bust shaping, (5 ch, 1 dc into next lp) 5 times, 5 ch, 1 dc into same ch as next join, (5 ch, 1 dc over next trip tr) 4 times, 5 ch, 1 dc into next ch sp, (5 ch, 1 dc over next trip tr) 4 times, 1 dc into same ch as next ss, (5 ch, 1 dc into next lp) 31 times, 5 ch, 1 dc into top of next tr, (5 ch, 1 dc into next 5 ch lp) 4 times, 5 ch, 1 dc over next tr, (5 ch, 1 dc into next 5 ch lp) 4 times, 5 ch, 1 dc into same ch as base of next tr (5 ch, 1 dc into next lp) 5 times, 2 ch, 1 tr into next dc, 1 ch, turn.

4th Size Only
Next Row: With right side facing attach thread to last dc made on last row before bust shaping, (5 ch, 1 dc into next lp) 6 times, 5 ch, 1 dc into same ch as next join, (5 ch, 1 dc over next trip tr) 3 times, 5 ch, ★ over next trip tr work 1 dc 5 ch and 1 dc, (5 ch, 1 dc over next trip tr) twice, 5 ch; rep from ★ once more, 1 dc into same ch as next ss, (5 ch, 1 dc into next lp) 31

times, 5 ch, 1 dc into top of next tr, ★★ (5 ch, 1 dc into next 5 ch lp) twice, 5 ch, into next 5 ch lp work 1 dc 5 ch and 1 dc; rep from ★★ once more, (5 ch, 1 dc into next 5 ch lp) 3 times, 5 ch, 1 dc into same place as base of next tr, (5 ch, 1 dc into next lp) 6 times, 2 ch, 1 tr into next dc, 1 ch, turn.

All Sizes
Work in patt for 6 rows turning with 5 ch at end of last row.
Rep 7th and 8th rows of back once. Work in patt for 26 rows more or for length required. Fasten off.
Join back and front together by sewing right side seam. Sew left side seam for 8 cm (3½in) from top leaving remainder of seam open.

Top Edging
1st Row: With right side facing attach thread to first lp made on last row of front, 5 dc into same lp, 5 dc into each lp, 1 ss into first dc.
2nd Row: 1 ss into next dc ★ 1 dc into next dc, 8 ch, miss 9 dc; rep from ★ ending with 1 ss into first dc.
3rd Row: Into each lp work 3 dc (3 ch, 2 dc) twice 3 ch and 2 dc, 1 ss into first dc. Fasten off.

Lower Edging
1st Row: With right side facing attach thread to top of last dbl tr made on 1st row of back, 1 dc into same place as join, 4 dc over each dbl tr along lower edge, 1 dc into same ch as first dbl tr made on 1st row of front, 1 ch, turn.
3rd and 4th rows form patt.
Work in patt for 2 rows more turning with 5 ch at end of last row.
7th Row: 1 dc into 2 ch sp, ★ 5 ch, 1 dc into next lp; rep from ★ ending with 5 ch, 1 dc into turning ch lp, 2 ch, 1 tr into 3rd of 5 turning ch, 1 ch, turn.
8th Row: 1 dc into first tr, ★ 5 ch, 1 dc into next 5 ch lp; rep from ★ to within turning ch, 5 ch, 1 dc into 3rd of 5ch, turn.
Work in patt for 7 rows more turning with 5 ch at end of last row.
Rep last 9 rows 4 times more then 7th and 8th rows again.
Work in patt for 26 rows more omitting turning ch at end of last row. Fasten off.

Front
Work as back for 44 rows omitting turning ch at end of last row, turn. Fasten off.

Detail from the crocheted lace Flower Dress bodice

Bust Shaping

1st Row: Miss first 3 (4, 5, 6) lps of previous row, attach thread to centre ch of next lp, ★ 5 ch, 1 dc into next lp; rep from ★ to within last 4 (5, 6, 7) lps, 2 ch, 1 tr into centre ch of next lp, 5 ch, turn.

2nd Row: ★ 1 dc into next 5 ch lp, 5 ch; rep from ★ to within last 2 lps, 1 dc into next lp, 1 trip tr into centre ch of next lp, 5 ch, turn.

3rd Row: ★ 1 dc into next lp, 5 ch; rep from ★ to within last 2 lps, 1 dc into next lp, 2 ch, 1 tr into next dc, 5 ch, turn.

Rep 2nd and 3rd rows 5 (6, 7, 8) times more.

Next Row: ★ 1 dc into next 5 ch lp, 5 ch; rep from ★ to within last 5 ch lp, 1 ss into centre ch of next lp. Fasten off.

1st and 2nd Sizes Only

Next Row: With right side facing attach thread to last dc made on last row before bust shaping, (5 ch, 1 dc into next lp) 3, (4) times, 5 ch, 1 dc into same ch as next join, (5 ch, 1 dc over next trip tr) 6 (7) times, 5 ch, 1 dc into same ch as next ss, (5 ch, 1 dc into next lp) 31 times, 5 ch, 1 dc into top of next tr, (5 ch, 1 dc into next 5 ch lp) 6, (7) times, 5 ch, 1 dc into same ch as base of next tr, (5 ch, 1 dc into next lp) 3, (4) times, 2 ch, 1 tr into next dc, 1 ch, turn.

2nd Row: 1 dc into each dc, 1 ch, turn.

3rd Row: 1 dc into each of first 3 dc, ★ 3 ch, 1 dc into each of next 4 dc; rep from ★ omitting 1 dc at end of last rep. Fasten off.

Strap (make 2)

1st Row: Commence with 4 ch, 1 dbl tr into 4th ch from hook, ★ 3 ch, 1 dbl tr into top of last dbl tr; rep from ★ 65 times more or for length required to fit over shoulder.

2nd Row: Over each dbl tr to within last dbl tr work 2 dc 3 ch and 2 dc, into next lp work 2 dc 3 ch 5 dc 3 ch and 2 dc, into each lp to within last lp along other side of 1st row work 2 dc 3 ch and 2 dc, into next lp work 2 dc 3 ch and 3 dc, 1 ss into first dc. Fasten off.

Damp and pin out to shape.

First Spray – Large Flower, First Petal
Commence with 10 ch.

1st Row (right side): 1 dc into 2nd ch from hook, 1 dc into each of next 7 ch, 3 dc into next ch, 1 dc into each ch along opposite side of foundation ch, 3 ch, 1 ss into back lp of first dc (base of petal).

2nd Row: 1 dc into same place as ss, working into back lp only of each dc work 1 dc into each of next 7 dc, 2 dc into each of next 3 dc, 1 dc into each dc, 3 ch, turn.

3rd Row: Miss first 3 dc,' (1 dc into next dc, 3 ch, miss 2 dc) twice, 1 dc into next dc, 5 ch, (miss 2 dc, 1 dc into next dc, 3 ch) 3 times, miss 2 dc, 1 ss into next dc. Fasten off.

Second Petal
Work as first petal for 2 rows turning with 1 ch instead of 3 ch at end of last row.

3rd Row: 1 ss into last lp made on previous petal, 1 ch, miss first 3 dc on second petal, 1 dc into next dc and complete as first petal.

Make 3 more petals joining each as second petal was joined to first turning with 1 ch at end of last petal. Do not fasten off.

Edging
Into each of next 3 lps work 1 dc 1 half tr 2 tr 1 hlf tr and 1 dc (3 shells made), ★ into next lp work 1 dc 1 hlf tr 4 tr 1 hlf tr and 1 dc, a shell into next lp, 1 dc into next lp, 1 dc into first free lp on next petal, a shell into next lp; rep from ★ 4 times more omitting 2 dc and a shell at end of last rep, a shell into each of next 2 lps. Fasten off.

Centre
1st Row: With right side facing attach thread to 3 ch lp at base of first petal made, 1 dc into same place as join, (3 ch, 1 dc into base of next petal) 4 times, 3 ch, remove lp from hook, insert hook into first dc and draw dropped lp through.

2nd Row: Into last sp made work 2 dc, 7 ch, remove lp from hook, insert hook into last dc made and draw dropped lp through (a joining st made), 9 dc into lp just made, 1 ss into same place as joining st (a ring made), into same sp work 2 dc a ring and 1 dc, into each sp work (2 dc, a ring) twice and 1 dc, 1 ss into first dc. Fasten off.

Stem
Commence with 31 ch.
1st Row: 1 dc into 2nd ch from hook, 1 dc into each ch to within last ch, 3 dc into next ch, working along other side of foundation ch, 1 dc into each of next 16 ch, 14 ch, a joining st into last dc, into lp just made work (3 dc, 3 ch) 5 times and 3 dc, 1 ss into same place as joining st, 1 dc into each ch.

Fasten off.

Flower Bud
Commence with 31 ch.
1st Row: 1 dc into 2nd ch from hook, 1 dc into each ch to within last ch, 3 dc into next ch, 1 dc into each ch along opposite side of foundation ch to within last ch, 2 dc into next ch, working into back lp of each dc work 1 dc into each of next 9 dc, 1 ch, turn. Continue to work into back lp only of each dc.

2nd Row: 1 dc into each of first 8 dc, 2 dc into each of next 3 dc, 1 dc into each of next 8 dc, 1 ch, turn.

3rd Row: 1 dc into each of first 10 dc, 2 dc into each of next 2 dc, 1 dc into each dc, 1 ch, turn.

4th Row: 1 dc into each dc. Fasten off.

Centre
Commence by winding thread 10 times round end of crochet hook and remove from hook.
1st Row: Into ring work (2 dc, 11 ch, a joining st into last dc, 15 dc into lp just made, 1 ss into same place as last joining st) 3 times and 4 dc, 1 ss into first dc. Fasten off.

Sew centre in position to flower bud. Sew flower in position to one end of stem and stem of bud to opposite end.

Make 17 more sprays or number desired.

Second Spray – Large Flower
Commence by winding thread 30 times round the end of a pencil and remove from pencil.
1st Row: 20 dc into ring, 1 ss into first dc.

2nd Row: 1 dc into same place as ss, ★ 8 ch, miss 3 dc, 1 dc into next dc; rep from ★ ending with 8 ch, 1 ss into first dc.

3rd Row: Into each lp work 1 dc 1 hlf tr 7 tr 1 hlf tr and 1 dc, 1 ss into first dc.

4th Row: ★ (1 dc into next st, 3 tr into next tr) 4 times, 1 dc into next st, 1 ss into each of next 2 dc; rep from ★ omitting 1 ss at end of last rep. Fasten off.

Half Flower
Work as large flower for 1 row.
2nd Row: 1 dc into same place as ss, (8 ch, miss 3 dc, 1 dc into each of next 3 dc) twice, 8 ch, miss 3 dc, 1 dc, into next dc, 1 ch, turn.

3rd Row: ★ Into next lp work 1 dc 1 hlf tr 7 tr, 1 hlf tr and 1 dc, 1 dc into each of next 3 dc; rep from ★ 3 times omitting 3 dc at end of last rep, 1 ss into next dc, turn.

4th Row: 1 ss into next dc, ★ (1 dc into next st, 3 tr into next st) 4 times, 1 dc into next st, miss 1 dc, 1 dc into each of next 2 dc, 3 ch, 1 ss into last dc (a p made), 1 dc into next dc, miss 1 dc; rep from ★ once more, (1 dc into next st, 3 tr into next st) 4 times, 1 dc into next st, 1 ss into next dc, 1 ss into next free dc, 35 ch, 1 hlf tr into 3rd ch from hook (base of stem), 1 hlf tr into each of next 16 ch, 20 ch, 1 hlf tr into 3rd ch from hook, 1 hlf tr into each of next 17 ch, 1 hlf tr into same ch as next hlf tr, 1 hlf tr into each of next 16 ch, miss 1 dc, 1 ss into next dc. Fasten off.

Shamrock
Commence with 28 ch.
1st Row: 1 ss into 8th ch from hook, (7 ch, 1 ss into same place as last ss) twice, 1 dc into each of next 19 ch, 3 dc into next ch, working along opposite side of foundation ch work 1 dc into each of next 19 ch (stem completed), into each lp work 1 dc 1 hlf tr 9 tr 1 hlf tr and 1 dc (shamrock completed), 1 ss into next dc. Fasten off.
Sew stem of shamrock to base of stem on half flower. Sew flower in position to remaining point of stem. Make 17 more sprays or number desired.

Single Small Flower
Commence by winding thread 10 times round the end of crochet hook and remove from hook.
1st Row: 10 dc into ring, 1 ss into first dc.
2nd Row: 1 dc into same place as ss, ★ 4 tr into next dc, 1 dc into next dc; rep from ★ ending with 4 tr into next dc, 1 ss into first dc. Fasten off.
Make 21 more small flowers or number desired.

Single Large Flower
Commence by winding thread 30 times round the end of a pencil and remove from pencil.
1st Row: 20 dc into ring, 1 ss into back lp of first dc.
2nd Row: 1 dc into same place as ss, working into back lp only of each dc, ★ miss 1 dc, 7 tr into next dc, miss 1 dc, 1 dc into next dc; rep from ★ omitting 1 dc at end of last rep, 1 ss into first dc. Fasten off.
Make 27 more large flowers or number desired.

Large Leaf
Commence with 25 ch.
1st Row: 1 dc into 2nd ch from hook, 1 dc into each ch to within last ch, 3 dc into next ch (tip of leaf), 1 dc into each ch along opposite side of foundation ch, 1 dc into same place as last dc (base of leaf). Hereafter pick up back lp only of each dc, 1 dc into each dc to within 4 dc from centre dc at tip of leaf, 1 ch, turn.
2nd Row: 1 dc into each dc to within centre dc at base of leaf, 3 dc into next dc, 1 dc into each dc on other side to within 4 dc from centre dc at tip of leaf, 1 ch, turn.
3rd to 7th Row: 1 dc into each dc to within centre dc of 3 dc group at base of leaf, 3 dc into next dc, 1 dc into each dc on other side to within last 3 dc, 1 ch, turn.
8th Row: 1 dc into each dc to within last 3 dc. Fasten off.
Make 15 more large leaves or number desired.

Small Leaf
Commence with 21 ch.
Work as large leaf for 5 rows.
6th Row: As 8th row of large leaf.
Make 19 more small leaves.

Finishing
Dampen the crochet and pin out to shape and to the measurements. Leave to dry. Sew the motifs to the ground in the arrangement shown in the picture, or as desired. Sew the straps to the bodice edge.

Making up the dress
Hand-sew the zip fastener into the bodice from the top edge to within 25mm (1in) of the waist edge.

Cut the skirt fabric into two pieces of the desired length plus 25mm (1in) for a narrow hem, plus 12mm (½in) for the waist seam. Place the two pieces together, right sides facing, and machine-stitch the side seams, leaving the left side seam open at the top edge for 20 cm (8in). Run two rows of gathering stitches round the top edge and pull up the gathering to fit the lower edge of the bodice. Trim the seam allowance and then neaten the gathered edge with seam binding. Place the bodice over the neatened waist edge and hand-sew in position. Complete the insertion of the zip fastener. Work a narrow hem on the bottom edge of the skirt.

Irish crochet motifs used on the Flower Dress bodice

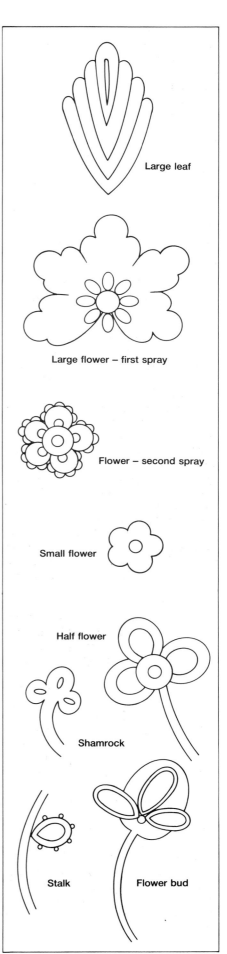

Large leaf

Large flower – first spray

Flower – second spray

Small flower

Half flower

Shamrock

Stalk

Flower bud

VINE LEAVES IN IRISH CROCHET

The antique crocheted lace collar is a typical pattern of the late nineteenth century. Irish crochet patterns used all kind of plant forms and the vine provided some very workable shapes. The edge of the collar has been adapted from a Venetian lace edging.

The method of working for this type of crochet was different from that worked today. Because it developed from observation of needle lace, pieces were assembled in a similar way.

The pattern was first drawn on glazed cotton fabric, with the motifs, the edges and the ground lines marked.

The motifs and the edges were then worked. The thread used was quite fine and a cording thread was used as an inner core over which stitches were made. This added strength to the lace and made the ridge lines more pronounced. These motifs were then basted to the pattern with the edge, and the chain bars were worked from motif to motif and motif to edge, following the drawn pattern. Sometimes, the motifs were joined with needlemade bars with picots and the effect was even more like needle lace.

The finished lace was finally released from the glazed cotton pattern.

The vine leaves and grapes motif has been abstracted from the collar opposite

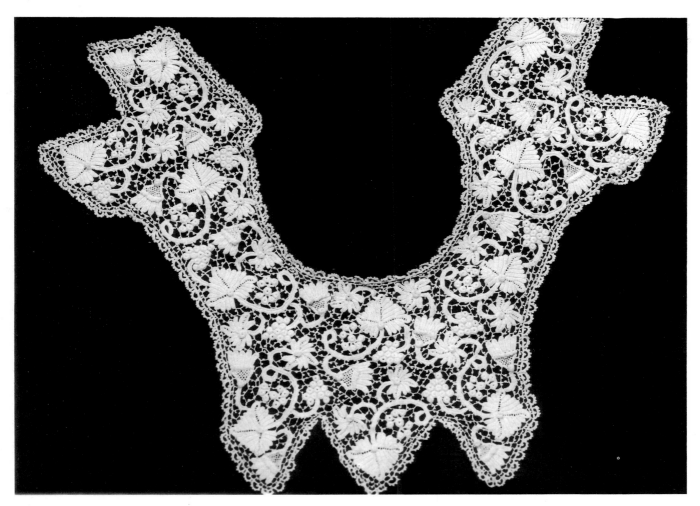

Materials required

For one motif: 1 20g ball of Coats Chain-Mercer Crochet cotton No 40

Crochet hook 1.00mm (No 4)

Tension

11 loops – 7.5cm (3in), 8 rows 25mm (1in).

Abbreviations

ch – chain; dc - double crochet; hlf tr – half treble; tr – treble; dbl tr – double treble; lp(s) – loop(s); st – stitch; ss – slip stitch; p – picot; rep – repeat; sp – space; patt – pattern.

Grapes

Wind the thread 10 times round the end of the crochet hook and remove from the hook.

Work 12 dc into the ring, 1 ss into first dc.

Make 16 more rings in this way and sew them together.

Grape leaves

These consist of a large leaf and two small leaves worked from the dress bodice (pattern on pages 84–87) with 2 very small leaves worked as follows:

Commence with 12 ch.

Work as for large leaf for three rows.

4th Row: As for 8th row of large leaf.

Stem

Commence with 31 ch.

1st Row: 1 dc into 2nd ch from hook, 1 dc into each ch to within last ch, 3 dc into next ch, working along other side of foundation ch, 1 dc into each of next 30 ch. Fasten off.

Finishing

Make vine leaves by joining 2 small leaves on either side of a large leaf and 2 very small leaves to each small leaf. Attach the stems to the grapes and leaves and sew into the required position on the place mat.

It is possible to vary the size of the leaves by changing the number of starting ch and to vary the number of grapes so that a composite edge can be made. Do not press Irish crochet unless absolutely necessary. It should be slightly raised and pressing will flatten it. Press only over a thick, soft pad or a towel.

Detail from the crocheted lace collar (above), showing a leaf and bunch of grapes

THE ROSE QUILT

The rose motif is one of the most loved of Irish crocheted lace patterns. It has raised petals, which provide a dimensional look to the lace. The motif given here is approximately 12.5cm (5in) square and sufficient squares can be made to apply to a single bed-sized quilt – you would require 160 motifs – or a smaller, cot-sized quilt could be made with just 42 motifs. If you prefer to work just a few motifs, make 9 for a beautiful cushion.

Materials required

Coats Chain-Mercer Crochet cotton No 40
9 20g balls for a cot quilt; 32 20g balls for a single quilt; 3 20g balls for a cushion
Crochet hook 1.00mm (No 4)

Tension

Finished size of individual motif, 12.5cm (5in) square approximately.

Abbreviations

ch – chain; dc – double crochet; hlf tr – half treble; tr – treble; dbl tr – double treble; trip tr – triple treble; st – stitch; lp(s) – loop(s); sp – space; ss – slip stitch; rep – repeat.

First Motif
Commence with 5 ch.
1st Row: 15 dbl tr into 5th ch from hook, 1 ss into 5th of 5 ch.
2nd Row: 1 dc into same place as ss, ★ 4 ch, miss 1 dbl tr, 1 dc into next dbl tr; rep from ★ ending with 4 ch, 1 ss into first dc.
3rd Row: Into each lp work 1 dc 1 hlf tr 5 tr 1 hlf tr and 1 dc, 1 ss into first dc.
4th Row: Working behind previous 2 rows, 1 ch, ★ 1 dc into next free dbl tr on 1st row, 6 ch; rep from ★ to end.
5th Row: Into each lp work 1 dc 1 hlf tr 7 tr 1 hlf tr and 1 dc, inserting hook from behind work 1 ss into first dc made on 4th row.
6th Row: Working behind previous row, 11 ch, ★ into next dc on 4th row work 1 dbl tr 7 ch and 1 dbl tr (a V st made), 7 ch, 1 dbl tr into next dc on 4th row, 7 ch; rep from ★ ending with a V st into next dc on 4th row, 3 ch, 1 dbl tr into 4th of 11 ch.
7th Row: 1 dc into lp just formed, ★ 4 ch, 1 dc into next lp, 7 ch, a V st into sp of next V st, 7 ch, 1 dc into next lp; rep from ★ omitting 1 dc at end of last rep, 1 ss into first dc.
8th Row: ★ Into next lp work 1 dc 3 ch and 1 dc, into each of next 3 lps work 1 dc 1 hlf tr 7 tr 1 hlf tr and 1 dc; rep from ★ ending with 1 ss into first dc

made on 7th row inserting hook from behind.
9th Row: Working behind previous row, 1 dc into same place as ss, ★ 5 ch, 1 dc into next dc on 7th row, (9 ch, 1 dc into next dbl tr on 7th row) twice, 9 ch, 1 dc into next dc on 7th row; rep from ★ omitting 9 ch and 1 dc at end of last rep, 4 ch, 1 trip t into first dc.
10th Row: 1 dc into lp just formed, ★ (9 ch, 1 dc into next lp) twice, 9 ch, into next lp work 1 dbl tr 9 ch and 1 dbl tr, 9 ch, 1 dc into next lp; rep from ★ omitting 9 ch and 1 dc at end of last rep, 4 ch, 1 trip tr into first dc.
11th Row: Into lp just formed work 1 dc 7 ch and 1 dc, ★ (5 ch, into next lp work 1 dc, 7 ch and 1 dc) 3 times, 5 ch, into next lp work 1 dc 9 ch and 1 dc, 5 ch, into next lp work 1 dc 7 ch and 1 dc; rep from ★ omitting 5 ch, 1 dc, 7 ch and 1 dc at end of last rep, 2 ch, 1 tr into first dc.
12th Row: 7 ch, ★ (1 dc into next 7 ch lp, 9 ch) 3 times, 1 dc into next 7 ch lp, 4 ch, 1 tr into next 5 ch lp, into next 9 ch lp work 7 dbl tr 3 ch and 7 dbl tr, 1 tr into next 5 ch lp, 4 ch; rep from ★ omitting 1 tr and 4 ch at end of last rep, 1 ss into 3rd of 7 ch.

Detail of the Rose Quilt motif

13th Row: 1 ss into each of next 2 ch, 1 dc into same lp, ★ 7 ch, 1 dc into next lp, into next lp work (1 dbl tr, 1 ch) 9 times and 1 dbl tr, 1 dc into next 1p, 7 ch, 1 dc into next lp, 7 ch, miss 3 dbl tr, 1 dc into next next dbl tr, 7 ch, into next lp work 1 dc 7 ch and 1 dc, 7 ch, miss 3 dbl tr, 1 dc into next dbl tr, 7 ch, 1 dc into next lp; rep from ★ omitting 7 ch and 1 dc at end of last rep, 3 ch, 1 dbl tr into first dc.

14th Row: 1 dc into lp just formed, ★ 9 ch, 1 dc into next lp, (1 dc into next 1 ch sp, 5 ch) 8 times, 1 dc into next 1 ch sp, 1 dc into next 1p, 9 ch, 1 dc into next lp, 9 tr into next 1p, into next 1p work 1 dc 5 ch and 1 dc, 9 tr into next lp, 1 dc into next lp; rep from ★ omitting 1 dc at end of last rep, 1 ss into first dc.

15th Row: 1 ss into next lp, 3 ch, 10 tr into same lp, ★ (1 dc into next lp, 3 ch) 7 times, 1 dc into next lp, 11 tr into next lp, miss 1 dc and 2 tr, 1 dc into next tr, 9 ch, into next lp work 1 dc 5 ch and 1 dc, 9 ch, miss 1 dc and 6 tr, 1 dc into next tr, 11 tr into next lp; rep from ★ omitting 11 tr at end of last rep, 1 ss into 3rd of 3 ch.

16th Row: 1 ss into each of next 4 tr, ★ 1 dc into next tr, 7 ch, 1 dc into next lp, (5 ch, miss next lp, 1 dc into next lp) 3 times, 7 ch, miss 1 dc and 5 tr, 1 dc into next tr, 7 ch, 9 tr into next lp, into next lp work 1 tr 7 ch and 1 tr, 9 tr into next lp, 7 ch, miss 1 dc and 5 tr; rep from ★ ending with 1 ss into first dc.

17th Row: ★ 7 dc into next lp, (into next lp woirk 1 dc 1 hlf tr 5 tr 1 hlf tr and 1 dc) 3 times, (7 dc into next lp) twice, 1 dc into next tr, 1 hlf tr into next tr, 1 tr into next tr, 1 dbl tr into each of next 7 tr, into next lp work 5 dbl tr 5 ch and 5 dbl tr, 1 dbl tr into each of next 7 tr, 1 tr into next tr, 1 hlf tr into next tr, 1 dc into next tr, 7 dc into next lp; rep from ★ ending with 1 ss into first dc. Fasten off.

Second Motif
Work as first motif for 16 rows.

17th Row: 7 dc into next lp, (into next lp work 1 dc 1 hlf tr 5 tr 1 hlf tr and 1 dc) 3 times, (7 dc into next lp) twice, 1 dc into next tr, 1 hlf tr into next tr, 1 tr into next tr, 1 dbl tr into each of next 7 tr, 5 dbl tr into next lp, 2 ch, 1 dc into corresponding lp on first motif, 2 ch, 5 dbl tr into same lp on second motif, 1 dbl tr into each of next 7 tr, 1 tr into next tr, 1 hlf tr into next tr, 1 dc into next tr, (7 dc into next lp) twice, into next lp work 1 dc 1 hlf tr 5 tr 1 hlf tr and 1 dc, into next

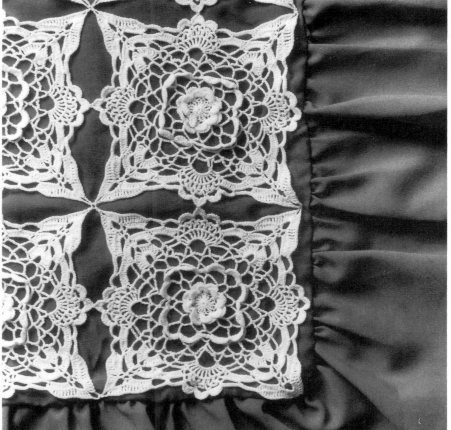

Joined motifs hand-sewn to a frilled quilt-cover

lp work 1 dc 1 hlf tr and 3 tr, 1 ss into corresponding tr on first motif, into same lp on second motif work 2 tr 1 hlf tr and 1 dc, into next lp work 1 dc 1 hlf tr 5 tr 1 hlf tr and 1 dc, (7 dc into next lp) twice, 1 dc into next tr, 1 hlf tr into next tr, 1 tr into next tr, 1 dbl tr into each of next 7 tr, 5 dbl tr into next lp, 2 ch, 1 dc into next 5 ch lp on first motif, 2 ch, 5 dbl tr into same lp on second motif and complete as first motif.

For a cot quilt, make 6 rows of 7 motifs joining each as second motif was joined to first. Where 4 corners meet join 3rd and 4th motifs to joining of previous motifs. To make a single bed-sized quilt, make 16 rows of 10 motifs. A cushion will need 3 rows of 3 motifs, for a 40cm (16in) square cushion cover.

Finishing
Dampen the finished crochet and pin out to shape and to measurements. Leave to dry.

Making a quilt
To make a quilt, cut two pieces of fabric to the desired size plus 5cm (2in) all round. Cut 3 pieces of wadding to the desired size of the finished quilt. Cut a piece of muslin to the same size as the wadding. Baste the 3 pieces of wadding to the muslin on the edges. Place the quilt top on the muslin side of the wadding, right side up, then lay the crochet on top. Working from the middle outwards, pin the crochet to the fabric. Hand-sew the crochet to the quilt, working tiny stitches through all thicknesses, round the outside edges of the crochet, then at the joining points of the motifs. If a frill is to be added to the quilt, join 25cm (10in) wide strips of fabric, to make twice the circumference of the quilt. Fold the frill, wrong sides together and press. Join the short ends. Gather the raw edges together. Baste the frill round the quilt, matching the raw fabric edges. Lay the quilt backing fabric on top, right sides facing. Baste all round. Machine-stitch along one-third of the first side, round the other three sides, then about one-third of first side again, leaving the middle third open. Unpick the basting threads. Turn the quilt to the right side through the open seam. Press lightly. Close the open seam with small slip-stitches.

IRISH LACE PINCUSHION

The velvet pincushion has a motif of crocheted lace applied to the top and a matching edging stitched to the sides. The motif could also be worked and applied to the corner of a tablecloth. The edging might be used to edge a trolley cloth, or a bed sheet. Both pieces are ideally suited for applying to bathroom towels.

Materials required

1 20g ball of Coats Chain-Mercer Crochet cotton No 40
Size 1.00mm (no 4) crochet hook
17×42cm (6¾×16½in) velvet fabric
Polyester filling for the pincushion
Sewing thread
Thin card

Tension

First 3 rows – 4cm (1⅝in) diameter.

Measurements

Motif 9cm (4½in) square
Edging 25mm (1in) deep
Pincushion, finished size; 10×10× 3cm (4×4×1¼in) approximately

Abbreviations

ch – chain; ss – slip stitch; dc – double crochet; tr – treble; dbl tr – double treble; trip tr – triple treble; lp – loop; rep – repeat; p – picot.

Motif

Commence with 32 ch, join with a ss to form a ring.

1st Row: 1 dc into same place as ss, 1 dc into each ch, 1 ss into first dc.

2nd Row: 3 ch, 1 tr into same place as ss, 2 tr into each dc, 1 ss into 3rd of 3 ch.

3rd Row: 1 dc into same place as ss, ★ 3 ch, miss 1 tr, 1 dc into each of next 3 tr; rep from ★ omitting 1 dc at end of last rep, 1 ss into first dc.

4th Row: 1 ss into next lp, 6 ch, 1 ss into 4th ch from hook – a p made, (1 tr into same lp, 3 ch, 1 ss into last tr – another p made) 4 times, 1 tr into same lp, remove lp from hook, insert hook into 3rd of first 6 ch and draw dropped lp through – a 5 p flower made, ★ 9 ch, into next lp work (1 tr, a p) 5 times and 1 tr, remove lp from hook, insert hook into 6th last tr made and draw dropped lp through – another 5 p flower made; rep from ★ ending with 4 ch, 1 trip tr into 3rd of 6 ch.

5th Row: 1 dc into lp just made, ★ 9 ch, 1 dc into next lp, 9 ch, 1 tr into next lp, 17 ch, 1 tr into next lp, 9 ch, 1 dc into next lp; rep from ★ omitting 9 ch and 1 dc at end of last rep, 4 ch, 1 trip tr into first dc.

6th Row: 1 dc into lp just made, ★ 5 ch, into next lp work (1 tr, a p) 5 times and 1 tr – a 5 p shell made, 5 ch, 1 dc into next lp, 5 ch, into next lp

Crocheted lace motif and edging mounted on a pincushion

work a 5 p shell 7 ch and a 5 p shell, 5 ch, 1 dc into next lp; rep from ★ omitting 5 ch and 1 dc at end of last rep, 2 ch, 1 tr into first dc.

7th Row: 1 dc into lp just made, ★ 5 ch, 1 dc into next lp, 5 ch, a 5 p flower into centre p on next shell, (5 ch, 1 dc into next lp) twice, 5 ch, a 5 p flower into centre p on next shell, 5 ch, into next lp work a 5 p flower 7 ch and a 5 p flower, 5 ch, a 5 p flower into centre p on next shell, 5 ch, 1 dc into next lp; rep from ★ omitting 1 dc at end of last rep, 1 ss into first dc. Fasten off.

Edging

1st Row: Commence with ★ 4 ch, 1 dbl tr into 4th ch from hook; rep from ★ 49 times more, 1 ss into first commencing ch.

2nd Row: 1 ss into first lp, 6 ch, complete 5 p flower as before, ★ 5 ch, 1 dc into next lp, 5 ch, a 5 p flower into next lp; rep from ★ ending with 5 ch, 1 dc into last lp, 2 ch, 1 tr into 3rd of 6 ch.

3rd Row: 1 dc into lp just made, ★ 5 ch, 1 dc into next lp; rep from ★ ending with 5 ch, 1 ss into first dc. Fasten off.

4th Row: Attach thread to first lp on opposite side of first row, 1 dc into same lp, ★ 5 ch, a 5 p flower into next lp, 5 ch, 1 dc into next lp; rep from ★

omitting 5 ch and 1 dc at end of last rep, 2 ch, 1 tr into first dc.

5th Row: As 3rd row of edging.

Finishing

Dampen the finished crochet and pin out on a board to shape and the measurements given. Leave to dry.

Making the pincushion

From the velvet fabric, cut a top and a base 12cm (4¾in) square. Cut the side section 5×42cm (2×16½in).

Join the short ends of the side section, right sides facing, with machine-stitching. Stitch one long side to the top piece, right sides facing and taking 1cm (½in) seams. Clip into the edges of the side section to fit the corners the top piece neatly. Trim the seam allowances.

Cut a piece of thin card 2.5×40cm (1×16in),

Score the card and bend at 10cm (4in) intervals. Join the short ends with tape to fit inside the pincushion. Turn the edges of the fabric onto the card and glue in place.

Make the base Cut a piece of card 10cm (4in) square. Glue it lightly to the remaining piece of velvet. Turn the edges of the fabric onto the card and glue. Stuff the pincushion firmly.

Hand-sew the base to the pincushion.

Catch the crocheted lace to the pincushion (see picture).

Displaying lace motifs

Pincushions, such as the one pictured, are an ideal way of displaying small pieces of lace. They have always been a decorative accessory since they first came into existence in the sixteenth century. Pins, which were expensive to buy, were usually stored in pretty pin boxes and were put onto a cushion for immediate use. Pincushions were treasured and often given as gifts for birthdays, engagements, weddings and Christenings. They were commonly made of luxurious fabrics, velvet or brocade and, in Victorian times, were lavishly embellished with lace.

Many of the motifs in this book can be used for decorating pincushions – here are a few: Broderie Anglaise edges, Reticella squares, Geometric needle lace butterflies, Teneriffe wheels, Point de Gaze flowers, Point de Venise edging and motifs, Tape lace flowers, Carrickmacross flowers or leaves, Filet motifs and Irish crochet flowers.

Catch the lace to the surface of the pincushion or fix it in place with fancy-headed pins.

The Care of Lace

Whether you have a collection of old laces, or you are a maker of lace – and often the two interests go together – you will be concerned that the beauty of the fabric is maintained and preserved.

The type of lace determines the use to which it will be put, and this can sometimes influence the way it is handled and laundered.

Richelieu
If the cutwork has been carefully worked and the raw edges of fabric closely Buttonhole-stitched, Richelieu will launder quite well. This lace can, therefore, be used both on household linens and clothing. It should be hand-washed in mild detergent or soap solution, dried and carefully ironed. Items carrying this lace can be put into a washing machine if they are first tied into a cloth bag or a pillow-case.

Broderie Anglaise
This stands up to laundering extremely well and can safely be used on clothes, including items which are frequently washed such as under-wear. Hand-wash, or machine-wash, tied into a bag or pillowcase. Broderie Anglaise can be starched to give it a crisp finish, and then ironed on the wrong side.

Ayrshire work
This is more delicate and should only be hand-washed. Dry the lace naturally and iron smooth on the wrong side, over a padded surface.

Drawn thread lace
Traditionally this has always been used for household linens because it washes well. Old pieces should be hand-washed, using a mild liquid detergent or a soap solution. Modern pieces, made from fabrics which may be of mixed fibres and worked with modern threads, can be machine-washed, but take the precaution of putting the item into a bag or pillow-case, to prevent the pulling of threads. Dry, starch and iron in the usual way.

Needle lace
This is surprisingly strong and can be washed but attention should be given to the thread from which the lace was made. Silk does not wash as well as cotton or linen threads.

Hand-wash needle lace in a mild liquid detergent. Rinse carefully, roll in a towel and then pin out the lace to shape on a board and leave to dry naturally. Do not iron needle lace.

If needle lace has been made for inserting into fabric, like fibres should be used so that they launder in the same way – ie cotton thread with cotton fabrics, linen thread with linen.

Tape lace
This is more delicate than most needle laces, but if care is taken, it can be washed in the same way as needle lace.

Limerick
This lace launders quite well. Hand-wash in a mild liquid detergent, rinse, roll in a towel and then pin out to dry naturally. If it requires ironing, iron on the wrong side over a padded surface.

Carrickmacross
This lace does not launder well because the technique makes the edges of the organdie to the net very weak and the purled edge can come away. With extreme care, it can be washed up to about ten times without damage. Wash by hand in a mild liquid detergent, pin out to dry naturally and iron, if necessary, on the wrong side. Carrickmacross lace dry-cleans well.

Filet
This is a strong lace and washes very well. Hand-wash or machine-wash, placing the item in a bag or a pillow-case.

Crochet
Crochet washes extremely well and keeps its shape. Wash by hand or in a washing machine, putting the item into a bag or pillowcase. Pin out to dry naturally but do not iron. If points or scallops appear to need ironing, do this on the wrong side over a padded surface.

Antique lace
Old lace, of any type, is usually made of fine thread and is sometimes fragile with age. It is often very dirty and, sometimes, has been dyed with coffee or tea, a favourite practise to obtain the ecru colour that was popular in the late nineteenth and early twentieth centuries.

It is inadvisable to wash old lace unless it is so bad that its beauty is lost. In its original state, the lace was probably a creamy colour. If it is washed, it may come out unnaturally white and this will not only look wrong but the lace will have lost some of its value.

Coffee and tea dye will not come out in anything but a mild detergent and then often patchily, so it is better to leave well alone.

Washing should be done by hand in distilled or soft water, using a pure soap or liquid detergent. Soak the lace in cold distilled or soft water first; this sometimes floats off some of the dust. Wash in hand-hot suds. Do not rub, but use a gentle, up and down movement, lifting the lace in the water. Rinse in warm, distilled water several times until every vestige of soap or detergent has been rinsed out.

Pin out the lace and dry naturally.

Iron mould marks can sometimes be removed by dabbing the mark gently with a little fresh lemon juice, afterwards drying the lace in sunlight.

Store antique laces in acid-free tissue paper. Do not fold the lace but roll it over card or tissue. Pad sleeves or bonnets with tissue to prevent wear in the creases.

Lace should never be stored in polythene bags.

Techniques for using lace
Lace insertions
Strips of lace or motifs, intended for inserting into fabric, should be made from thread similar to the ground fabric.

Lace may be attached on all sides or, as when used on a neckline, on three sides with the fourth side becoming the neckline.

The most satisfactory stitch for attaching lace is the three-sided stitch called Triangular Lace stitch or Point Turc. The stitch can be used on any type of fabric and on straight or curved edges.

Triangular Lace stitch
Baste the lace to the ground fabric, in position, on the right side, using a soft basting thread.

Work lace stitch using the same thread as that used for making the lace.

The stitch is worked from right to left, and the lower straight stitch is worked through the fabric and the top straight stitch into the lace.

The size of the stitch depends on the ground fabric; use small stitches when working on fine fabrics and larger stitches on heavier fabrics.

If a fairly large needle is used and the work is pulled slightly on every stitch, a decorative pattern of holes will form below the edge of the lace.

When the embroidery stitches round the lace have been completed, carefully cut away the fabric under the lace, working from the wrong side. Cut close to the stitches. If the ground fabric is likely to fray overcast the fabric edge to neaten.

If the item is likely to be laundered often, such as table linen, a zigzag machine-stitch can be used to apply the lace but the result is somewhat stiffer.

Attaching lace edges
Lace edgings can be attached to fabric using Triangular Lace stitch, afterwards cutting the fabric back to the stitching, and oversewing the fabric edge if required.

If the fabric edge is already finished, such as on a bought handkerchief, attach the lace by whipping it to the edge, using small stitches.

Edges of broderie Anglaise are usually attached with machine-stitching, using either straight stitch or zigzag stitch.

Lace appliqué
If lace motifs are being used as appliqué, attach the lace with small slip stitches.

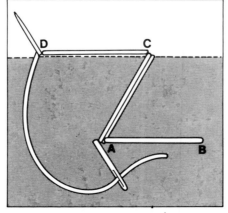

Fig 1 *Make a small Back stitch in the fabric at the left and bring the needle out at A, insert it at B, and bring the needle out again at A.*

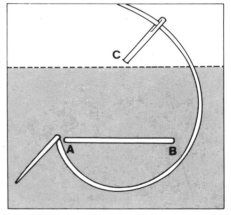

Fig 2 *Insert the needle at C into the lace, and bring it out at A.*

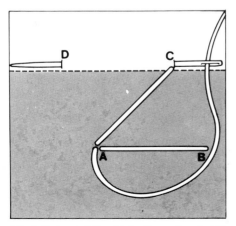

Fig 3 *Re-insert at C and bring the needle out at D.*

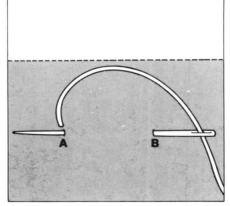

Fig 4 *Re-insert at C and bring needle out at D, re-insert at A and bring needle out at D.*

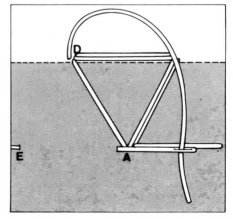

Fig 5 *Insert needle at A and bring it out at E, the distance between A-B to the left.*

Bibliography

Lace, a History, Santina Levey (Maney, 1983).
Victorian Lace, Patricia Wardle (Bean, 1982).
The Romance of Lace, Mary Eirwen Jones
  (Spring Books).
Hispanic Lace and Lacemaking, F. L. May
(Hispanic Society of America, 1939)

Suppliers' addresses

NET
Romance Bridals Ltd
12 D'Arblay Street
London W1 (mail order only)

TAPE
The English Lace School
Honiton Court
Rockbeare
Near Exeter, Devon

THREADS, CARRICKMACROSS SCISSORS
Mace & Nairn,
89 Crane Street
Salisbury SP1 2PY
Wiltshire

The Royal School of Needlework
25 Princes Gate
Kensington
London SW7

The Needlewoman
21 Needless Alley
Birmingham B2 5AE

North American Suppliers

Lacis
2982 Adeline Street
Berkeley
CA 94703
Tel: (415) 843 7178

Robbins Bobbins
Route 1
Box 1736
Mineral Bluff
GA 30559
Tel: (404) 374 6916

Index